Sonoma & Mendocino

SONOMA & MENDOCINO

Wine Tour

Artwork by

Sebastian Titus

Written by

Patricia Latimer / Deborah Kenly / Michael Topolos

A Vintage Image Book

Table of Contents

Historical

Perspective

To the north of San Francisco is a land of golden hills, rushing streams and grassy valleys. As a vast and relatively undeveloped frontier, the 5,085 square mile Sonoma-Mendocino region often seems forgotten by the people of California and the historians who write about it. Throughout its development, the area has been deeply bound to the history of California and an unusual mixture of Indians, homesteaders, gold diggers, freebooters, soldiers, conquistadors and oenophiles. It was here California was born.

In 1542, Juan Rodriquez, a celebrated Portugese adventurer, departed Navidad, a small port south of Puerta Vallerta in Mexico, on an exploratory voyage along the coast of California. Somehow never seeing the Golden Gate, he found Point Concepcion, Point Reyes and finally Cape Mendocino further up the California coast. He christened his last stop in honor of the Mexican-based patron, Viceroy Antonio de Mendoza. Thus today this area bears the familiar county and village name, Mendocino.

More than 200 years later in 1775, navigator of the Spanish navy, Lt. Juan Francisco de la Bodega Y Quadra, anchored his ship, the Sonora, in a well-protected coastal bay which would later become Bodega Bay in Sonoma County.

Meanwhile in 1776, a group of Catholic missionaries from Mexico embarked on one of the first overland exploratory expeditions into the area north of San Francisco. There they found a series of Pomo, Miwok and Wappo Indian settlements which were scattered throughout the more fertile regions. Long before the missionaries arrived, the aboriginal Indians had made the Sonoma-Mendocino wilderness their home.

Around 1799, the Russians founded a fur trading colony in Sitka, Alaska. Difficulties arose by 1806 when the Czarist settlers were faced with acute shortages of basic supplies which were insufficient to maintain the colony. So bad were the conditions that Nicolai Rezanof, the imperial inspector of the colony, looked to California for new sources of food.

It was not until 1809, however, that a group of Russians led by Alexander Kushoff explored the areas now known as Sonoma and Mendocino counties. Establishing the first permanent settlement north of San Francisco in 1812, the Russians located themselves above a natural harbor 30 miles north of Bodega Bay and 13 miles northwest of the mouth of the Russian River. Once the site of a Pomo Indian village, the place was christened simply Ross, an archaic name for Russia. The Russians were the first to cultivate grape vines in the Sonoma region, using cuttings brought from the Black Sea area.

The Russians' attempt to establish a colony north of San Francisco threatened the Spanish authorities, who feared that the Russians wanted to gain control of all of California. As the southernmost settlement of the Czarist empire in North America, this appeared a true attempt to colonize what is now the western United States. The Russian occupation was a problem for Spain and Mexico until the colony was sold in 1841 to Captain John Sutter of Sacramento Valley fame.

California was a province of Spain until February 1821, when Mexico gained its independence from the motherland. Because of poor communications, nothing was really known of this situation in California. Although some government officials may have suspected it, word of the Independence move did not reach California Gov. Luis Arguello until almost a year later in January, 1822.

Whatever territorial intentions the Russians may have had for expansion, their plans were seriously challenged by the implacable wording of the Monroe Doctrine. In Dec. 23, 1823, President James Monroe asserted "that the American continents . . . are henceforth not to be considered as subjects for colonization by any European powers."

In that same year, the last of the Franciscan missions was built, Mission San Francisco de Solano. Originally there was no intention on the part of the Mexicans to found another mission, but several factors led to its establishment. Governor Arguello, the first Mexican governor born in California, was so disturbed by the Russian colonization efforts along the northern California coastline that he asked Father Jose´ Altimira to hurry his plan to establish the new facility in Sonoma. Arguello felt that the mission would not only extend the church's religious influence, but act as a counter-force to possible Russian adventurism.

The Mission San Francisco de Solano was the last in a series of Franciscan enclaves which taught the "heathen" Indians western religion, education and agriculture. Located on the King's Highway, the "Camino Real," the missions were situated a day's journey apart by horse and wagon and extended from San Diego to Sonoma in northern California.

The original Mission San Francisco de Solano was a rough, temporary wooden structure which was gradually replaced with a more permanent Spanish style building with adjacent wood and adobe structures as well as a granary.

In the decade following 1823, Mexico was faced with the problem of finding an effective permanent form of government for California. Territorial legislatures were set up, and Monterey was selected as the capital in Northern California. In that period, Gov. Jose´ Figueroa, a gentleman prominent in Mexican politics, replaced Gov. Arguello. Also concerned about the ever increasing size and strength of the Russian settlement, the new governor decided to take action against it.

Gov. Figueroa investigated the background of one Mariano Guadalupe Vallejo as a possible appointee to take command of the Mission San Francisco de Solano. Something of a child prodigy, Vallejo displayed an interest in religion, politics, and world affairs at an early age. At 15, he began his military service as a cadet in the Presidial Company of Monterey, and thus was launched an illustrious military career. Rising rapidly through the ranks to corporal, sergent and before long, ensign, he helped quell a variety of Indian uprisings and also led a surveying party north of San Francisco through unexplored wilderness regions.In 1831, Vallejo was named commander of the San Francisco Presidio.

After Vallejo toured the Russian settlement at Ft. Ross in 1833, he realized the economic potential and political importance of occupying the land north of San Francisco. Enthusiastically, he reported to his superiors that the grassy, stream-fed Santa Rosa Valley and other neighboring areas were ideal for great ranchos and large herds of cattle. That the Russians sought only a base for fur trade and food sources seemed like a problem that could be resolved.

A year later, Gov. Figueroa, under the orders of the Mexican government, issued the Decree of Secularization which overthrew the authority of the Franciscan fathers and divided the mission property among the Indians, the church and the public. Gov. Figueroa named Vallejo as the commander of the Pueblo de Sonoma and civilian administrator of secularization for the Mission San Francisco de Solano in 1834.

Vallejo's colonization program was firmly established by 1835. The town of Sonoma was designed around a central plaza with a church and other residential dwellings and commercial buildings. Although the new leader encouraged settlers to come to Sonoma, the town's development was slow.

Vallejo became a general under a rather bizarre set of circumstances in 1836 when Mexican Nicolas Gutierrez was appointed governor and there developed a strong local sentiment against officials imported from Mexico. Shortly after the new governor took office, he threatened to disolve the territorial legislature in Monterey. One of its leading members and opponents of such an idea was Alvarado Vallejo, the nephew of Mariano Vallejo, who with his cohort Jose' Castro, decided to prepare for their own rather personal revolution.

In great haste, Alvarado Vallejo headed to Sonoma, where he hoped to solicit the support of his uncle. Much to the young man's surprise, Mariano Vallejo was not in favor of revolution, but preferred preservation of peace on the northern frontier. Dismayed, but still determined, Alvarado left for Monterey. Half-way there, he decided to go ahead with the revolution, proclaiming it in. "Mariano Guadalupe Vallejo's name." With Castro's assistance, young Alvarado assembled an army of men, captured the town of Monterey and demanded Gov. Gutierrez's surrender. As head of the new government and president of the new legislature, Castro nominated the by-then Lt. Vallejo as the General of the free and sovereign state of California.

Vallejo's rather heavy handed but nonetheless charming personality stimulated a mixed reaction of admiration and hatred among his associates. Prior to his visit to Ft. Ross, Vallejo had been openly accused of cruelty to the Indians. However, his policy changed when he realized that, if he befriended the Indians, they would not only act as a deterrent against outside aggression, but be less likely to harass the new settlers Vallejo was encouraging to homestead in the northern frontier.

An article written in the *New York Herald* explains the tenor of the Mexican government at that time.

"The stupidity of the people and the selfishness and tyranny of their military officers and government have reduced Mexico to the lowest grade of degradation and infamy. The sun never shone on a more beautiful country and God of Nature never dispensed his favors to a greater degree than he has on this now unfortunate country. Yet not withstanding these natural advantages, Mexico from certain causes, is now the meanest and lowest in the category of nations. Her people are ruled with a rod of iron and sunk in imbecility and infamy. Her military leaders are the most despotic

Russian River Valley

and mercenary that ever exercised power; through effects of successive revolutions, all confidence of government is gone. She is without an army or navy and her coffers are empty. There is a never-ending struggle by a set of designing men to attain management of highest affairs and the only principal that guides them is self-aggrandizement.

When James K. Polk became president of the United States in 1845, he was determined to acquire California by purchase or seizure. At that time, war with Mexico was anticipated and considered by some a virtual certainty.

By 1846, American pioneer families had begun to cross the rugged Sierra Nevada in increasingly large numbers to settle much of California including many parts of Sonoma County. These early settlers were attracted by stories and promises of opportunity in the western lands. The pioneers were deeply disappointed when they realized they had been misled in their hopes. There was no prosperity; there was no free land. Instead the Americans found Gen. Vallejo, a ruthless Mexican officer ruling in a virtually despotic manner and using his vast military power to control the people.

The American settlers lived in an atmosphere which was exacerbated by the repeated onorous edicts of the Mexican government. Americans were prohibited from owning land. Another time, all "foreigners", namely Americans, were ordered expelled from the country and asked to leave their weapons behind. As the situation worsened, the normally peaceful immigrants finally rallied to defend their lands and their lives. The incidents thus provoked were the first of a se-

ries of confrontations which led to the Bear Flag Revolt on June 14, 1846, in which mostly American citizens rebelled against Mexican authority and tried to establish an independent republic.

Less than a year earlier, United States surveyor and explorer Captain J. C. Fremont and a group of 60-odd Indian guides surveyors, and mountain men including Kit Carson, were on an exploratory mission to discover a short, practical route across the mountains to the Pacific. When they arrived in Monterey, the capital of the northern frontier, Fremont and his men received a warm reception from Gen. Castro. Fremont even obtained permission from Castro to conduct further expeditions in northern California. However, Fremont failed to obey Castro's request to by-pass the more populated and settled areas. Whatever Fremont's motives may have been remain a source of historical controversy and have not been firmly clarified. What is known is that barely a week passed after the Monterey visit before Fremont received orders from Castro to leave California at once. Fremont refused to comply.

Almost simultaneously, word reached Fremont from Washington, D.C., to situate himself at some point convenient to land and naval forces due to arrive in and around San Francisco. War with Mexico seemed inevitable. Fremont returned to the Sacramento Valley, not far from Sonoma or San Francisco.

On June 14, 1846, in the early morning, a group of anti-Mexican settlers at the advice of Fremont, stole the horses of Francisco Circe, which he was collecting for the forces which Gen. Castro was establishing in case of fighting in the northern frontier. Soon after, the

Ancient Zinfandel Vine

Americans rode together to the town of Sonoma where they surrounded the palatial residence of Gen. Vallejo and seized him and members of his family.

The rebels organized and elected one William B. Ide as their leader and established their own independent republic, modeling their new government after Texas. In celebration, the victors raised their homemade flag, a piece of unbleached muslin decorated with a brown bear, and flew it for nearly a month in Sonoma.

News of the Bear Flag Revolt travelled to John Fremont at Sutter's fort. Apparently recognizing an opportunity to further his ever present political ambitions and and probably feeling somewhat obligated to look out for the welfare of the rebels at Sonoma, who he believed were in imminent danger of Mexican reprisal, Fremont moved his whole camp to Sonoma. The band of mountain men arrived in Sonoma on June 25. From that day on, with the implied consent of the Bear settlers, Fremont was in command.

On July 6, 1846, Commodore John D. Sloat of the U.S.S. Portsmouth arrived off the coast of Monterey with the news of the war between Mexico and the United States. Soon thereafter, the Stars and Stripes was raised on the American Customs House in Monterey and three days later Old Glory was flying a-top the mast in the Sonoma plaza.

The development of the wine and grape industry in Sonoma-Mendocino has played an important part in the California wine story. From 1850 to 1900, this region was the center of history and culture. It was settled by an influential and imaginative group of wine pioneers such as Gen. Mariano G. Vallejo, Col. Agoston Harasz-thy, Samuel Orr, Louis Finne and other individuals who not only participated in the growth of Sonoma-Mendocino, but who are responsible for the achievements of this great North Coast wine district.

The first agriculturists in Sonoma County were the Russians, who in 1812 came to California and established a permanent colony north of Bodega Bay where they planted vegetables, orchards and vineyards. The Russians' grape growing and winemaking activities indicated the potential of developing the grape culture in the northern part of the state.

In 1824, when Father Altimira came north to found the Mission San Francisco de Solano, he planted the very popular Mission grapes, the original grapes planted by the Franciscan fathers. They were used for making a rather harsh-tasting wine. Records found at the mission reveal that the first vineyards tended by the priests yielded enough grapes to produce 1000 gallons of wine.

After the Decree of Secularization was passed in 1834, the Mexican government gained control over the California missions. The vineyards which Father Altimira had planted were taken over by Gen. Vallejo, who as the commander of the Pueblo de Sonoma expressed more than a passing interest in wine. As a measure to improve the quality of the wine which he wanted to make, Gen. Vallejo replanted the old vineyards with newer Mission grapes. The result of his early winemaking efforts was a moderately pleasing red wine.

Gen Vallejo's dedication to growing grapes and making wine so inspired friends, relatives and neighbors many of them joined him and settled in Sonoma where they experimented with establishing the fruit culture. In 1839, the first woman to own and plant a vineyard in the Santa Rosa Valley was Senora de Carillo. In 1847, a gentleman by the name of Nicholas Carriger shipped new grape varieties from the East Coast called Muscats, Isabellas and Catawbas. His neighbor William Hill imported grape varieties such as Rose' of Peru, Italia, Black Hamburg and Golden Chasselas.

Although originally the settlement of Northern California was slow in developing, the unexpected discovery of gold in 1848 at James W. Marshall's mill in the foothills of the Sierra Nevada changed the complexion of California forever. Suddenly speculators came from around the world to seek great fortune. Their journeys took them inland to new and unexplored areas of the northern frontier. A short two years later, there were French, Italian, German, Spanish, Scottish and English settlers, all in search of gold. When the gold quest proved unrewarding, the immigrants turned to agriculture and viticulture. It wasn't until the late 1850's that the colonists became aware of the choice Sonoma-Mendocino land and the possibility of its development.

One of the most colorful personalities to settle in the Sonoma area was the dashing Col. Agoston Haraszthy de Moskea. Like Gen. Vallejo, Col. Haraszthy contributed to the development and knowledge of the wine industry in California. By importing grapes from Europe and making very high quality wines, he was able to convince members of the state legislature that California was capable of producing some of the best grapes in the world. The results of his experimental work in the vineyard and in the cellar in Sonoma not only proved his point, but, in the end, established the basis for a full-fledged grape and wine industry.

Col. Haraszthy was born on August 30, 1812 in Futtak, Hungary, to an aristocratic family. As a youngster, Agoston grew up in a time of political change when the Hungarian citizen was questioning the authority of the government particularly in respect to the rights of the individual. Experiencing a very conventional upbringing, the boy attended fine schools where the scholastic emphasis was on the law. By virtue of his station in life, he enlisted in the service of the royal guard, acting as executive secretary to the viceroy and living a country-gentlemanly way of life as a squire and grower.

In spite of these obvious advantages in life, Col. Haraszthy was a torn man. So sympathetic was he with the grievances of the commoners that he took up their cause and became a leader in the Hungarian nationalist movement. As the commoners' spokesman, he advocated liberty, justice and equality. Before long, his political activities provoked a reaction from the established powers and he had to flee his country for the States.

As one of the more talented individuals to come to America, Col. Haraszthy approached his new adventure with his characteristic enthusiasm. Barely settled, he wrote and published an informative book about America in Hungarian for the friends he had left behind. An instinctive entrepreneur, he carved a small empire out of the Wisconsin wilderness and founded Sauk City. There he built bridges, constructed roads, started schools, organized churches, entered politics and experimented in agriculture.

Unfortunately, Col. Haraszthy developed an asthmatic condition and in 1849 he left the cold winter-hot summer climate of Wisconsin for the sunnier and warmer climate of San Diego, California. Settling in the Mission Valley, Col. Haraszthy planted some of the first imported vines in the area. Involved in first local, then state politics, he served as sheriff, city marshal and state assemblyman.

In the late 1850's Col. Haraszthy moved north to San Francisco. As a wine grower in Crystal Springs near San Mateo, he imported and planted European varieties, but unfortunately he did not have much success. Heading farther north, he purchased an estate bordering on the Mission Dolores near San Francisco. Again, he had difficulties. The moist sea air and the cool summer fogs prevented his grapes from ripening properly, and he was forced to look for a more favorable location.

When Col. Haraszthy finally found a site in Sonoma County, he was convinced that the warm, sunny, dry climate was excellent for growing grapes. Selecting prime land, the suave promoter found a parcel of over 500 acres which was situated on the gently sloping hills of the Mayacamas Mountains. Very appropriately, he called his estate Buena Vista which means Beautiful View in Spanish. Surrounding the elegant villa he constructed were the vineyards, which were eventually made up of 85,000 vines of foreign and domestic varieties. At the time of Col. Haraszthy's relocation, Sonoma was fast becoming a major viticultural center.

Col. Haraszthy's contribution to the California wine industry lies in the depth and scope of his research, which was based on hitherto unpublished information. It was simplified and made available to the California grape grower. Firm in his convictions, Haraszthy believed in the pre-eminence of wine made from imported varieties. His reasoning was based on the results of experiments which showed that California had the finest climate, the best soil and the greatest growing season of any area in the world. In order that other wine growers could benefit from his knowledge, Col. Haraszthy published a comprehensive *Report on Grapes and Wine in California*. Later on he founded the Horticultural Society of Sonoma and wrote a book, *The Honored Guide of Grape Culture*.

Recognition of Haraszthy's work in the wine industry was brought to public attention when, in 1861, Gov. John G. Downey asked him to go to Europe. There, on behalf of the state of California, which was now interested in promoting the growth of the grape industry, the wine adventurer was to find sample cuttings of select varieties which could be grown at home. Delighted with his assignment, Col. Haraszthy left in June of that year. Staying for close to five months, he visited France, Italy, Germany, Spain and Russia. He returned with 200,000 plants of nearly 500 varieties. Due to the unfavorable political climate of the moment, namely Haraszthy's alleged support for Southern forces during the Civil War, the state legislature would not pay Col. Haraszthy for his trip. Thus he was forced to raise revenue and sell his plants to growers across the state.

As friendly neighbors, Gen. Vallejo and Col. Haraszthy enjoyed competing against each other in

Sonoma Valley

state and local fairs to see who could produce the most outstanding wines. From the beginning Vallejo's wines received the highest praise, but, as Col. Haraszthy became more skilled as a winemaker, he came up with some superior vintages. During one of the very early harvests at Buena Vista, Col. Haraszthy and his three sons Arpad (who studied wine and champagne making in France and later formed his own company), Attila and Gaza made 1000 gallons of wine. Pleased with their results, they sold it commercially for $2 a gallon.

It should be noted that Col. Haraszthy was by no means the first person to import foreign varieties to the United States. Europeans who had originally settled here had done so earlier and made fine wine besides. What Col. Haraszty did do was to make particular varieties more well-known.

At the end of that year, Sonoma County was the state's second largest wine district with 1,100,000 vines under cultivation. Los Angeles was first with 1,200,000 vines planted. The area known as the Sonoma Valley continued to develop as a center for the production of high quality, dry table wines. This growing interest in wine in Sonoma County attracted the interest and investment of winemakers from the major wine growing countries of the world.

Among the more famous wine growers who settled in the area were Emil Dresel and Jacob Gundlach, founders of the Gundlach Bundschu Wine Co. Dresel, who grew up in the town of Gisenheim on the Rhine, came from a German wine family. Gundlach, a native of Bavaria, had a father who was a hotel owner and wine grower. Together as partners they bought magnificent vineyards in the foothills of the Huichica Mountains near the town of Sonoma. The vineyard was called the Rhinefarm and provided grapes for the wine which was made at the winery for their San Francisco-based retail company, the Gundlach Bundschu Wine Co.

Another very important wine firm Kohler & Frohling established vineyards in Sonoma County in 1875. As early as 1854, Charles Kohler and John Frohling had founded their company in Los Angeles where they grew grapes and made wine. Also in that same year, they opened a small retail shop on Merchant St. in San Francisco. By 1860, the partners did so well that they started an agency in New York which distributed their California wines. By 1875 the firm purchased 800 acres of rolling countryside in Glen Ellen in the Sonoma Valley. The partners produced some of their finest dry table wines from their Tokay Vineyard made up of Mission, Muscat, Rose' of Peru, Golden Chasselas and Riesling. To store their wine, they constructed a stone winery, a distillery and sherry cellars. In 1910, this prime Glen Ellen property was sold to the then world-famous author, Jack London.

An intriguing name in California viticulture is Kanaye Nagasawa, the owner of the highly respected Fountain Grove Vineyard. Born of Japanese nobility, he reached his position as sole proprietor of the American firm by following the teachings of one Thomas Harris. A mystical prophet whom Nagasawa met in England, Harris led his students to live in religious colonies first in New York and later California.

In 1875, Harris purchased 1400 acres of land in the Santa Rosa Valley to be used as a dairy farm and vineyard. Planting fine strains of Zinfandel, Pinot Noir and Cabernet Sauvignon, he produced highly prized vines which were sold in the United States, Great Britain and Japan. Nagasawa became the owner in 1920 after Harris was forced to leave the area due to a scandal in the Santa Rosa religious colony. To this day, older vintages of Fountain Grove Vineyard wines are among some of the finest red wines Sonoma County has ever produced.

Extensive planting was the order of the day during the 1870's. By 1875, Sonoma County ranked as the number one producer in California with a production of 3,397,612 gallons. Los Angeles County which until then had always ranked number one, took second place with 3,238,900 gallons. As a result of this production glut, a year later wine was selling for the rock-bottom price of 10¢ a gallon.

By the early 1880's the economy had improved and Sonoma County was once again on the road to recovery. For most of the Sonoma vintners, these early years showed marked success. However, in the 1880's the ravages of pylloxera, an insect which destroys the roots of the grapevine, were being disastrously felt throughout the county (and the state). As early as 1873, pylloxera was found on Sonoma grapevines.

In the late 1870's Julius Dresel of the Gundlach-Bundschu Wine Co., did extensive experimental work in his vineyard at the Rhinefarm, grafting disease-prone vines onto pylloxera resistant rootstock. His work was instrumental in saving vineyards in that county and elsewhere.

In 1909, Carl Dresel, grandnephew of Julius Dresel, wrote George C. Husman, one of the gentlemen Leon D. Adams credits with arresting the pylloxera plague in California. This excerpt describes Julius Dresel's work with pylloxera.

"At this time (1875) the pylloxera valatrix had already begun to devastate the vineyards in the Sonoma Valley. Mr. Dresel with his characteristic energy worked day and night studying ways and means to combat the ravages of the pest. He soon came to the conclusion that ordinary methods of isolation, destruction of infested spots and chemical poisons were impracticable. He was of the belief that the only sure remedy consisted in finding a root that would not succumb to the attack of the louse (vine-pest). He was the first man in California to import wild roots from the Mississippi and Mission River bottom, plant them in his vineyards, and to test them thoroughly he planted them with the lice obtained from his diseased vines.

"The roots continued to thrive and verified his belief (that it was necessary to find a pylloxera-resistant rootstock). In the next few years, the entire vineyard died from the effect of the louse. As each block of vines disappeared, it was replanted with resistant roots and later grafted. The experiment was eminently successful. The first crop from vines grafted on resistant roots was pressed in 1878 and the same vines are bearing today, a period of 30 years.

From 1881 to 1895 owners of flourishing Sonoma County vineyards were selling their wine grapes and bulk wines for very low prices. Not only was the wine industry in a very precarious economic state, but the United States was in the middle of a depression. As a means of saving themselves from further ruin, several major wine firms joined together to form the California Wine Association. Composed primarily of wine merchants, the organization set out to improve the general standard of wine and stabilize grape prices. The California Wine Association achieved its goals by enforcing established grower-winery contracts for grapes at fixed prices. Four of the original seven wineries in the association were located in Sonoma: Kohler & Frohling, who owned vineyards in Glen Ellen; B. Dreyfus & Co., who owned the Goldstein Vineyards in the Sonoma Valley and Arpad Haraszthy & Co.

Not too much later a rival syndicate, the California Winemakers' Corporation was formed. It was headed by John H. Wheeler, with the support of two other Italian Swiss Agricultural Colony supporters, Andrea Sbarboro and Pietro Rossi. Composed primarily of wine growers, the organization tried to stimulate the economy by encouraging grape growers to sell their grapes (or bulk wine) not just to one firm like the California Wine Association, but to numerous wine firms.

As Sonoma County developed into a viticultural center, it was settled by groups of people of various nationalities and cultures. With them, these immigrants brought the wisdom, love and laughter, as well as the cherished customs of their European homelands. One of the largest and most influential groups were the Italians. Between 1890 and 1919 there was a large settlement of Italians who lived between Healdsburg and Cloverdale and devoted most of their energies to winemaking. Traditionally, these growers and vintners would sell their wine to San Francisco wine firms or the aforementioned co-operatives or syndicates. Undaunt-ed by the challenge of a new and sometimes strange land, these men worked hard creating their own American wine story. Some of the individuals who should be remembered are Giuseppe Mazzoni, Edward Seghesio, Andrew Sodini, John Foppiano, Samuele Sebastiani and others.

Prior to 1900, another group of immigrants established the French Colony in the rolling hills between Cloverdale and Asti. One Fred Vadon, now 80, and one of the last surviving members of the French Colony recalls the names of his childhood friends, all founders of their own wineries. They include his father Felician Vadon, Jules Leroux, Paul Leroux, Armand de Hay, Theodor de Hay, Louis Bee, Emil Bee, Gustave Provost and Ulysseus Zurcher.

In a very short time, these dedicated newcomers helped to lay the cornerstone of the Sonoma wine industry. Sonoma's chief claim to fame was as a producer of bulk wines (these are wines which are held in storage tanks prior to bottling or sale to another winery under another's label), however, some of the wineries bottled under their own label or private labels (wines to be sold by other wineries, wine shops or restaurants).

The turn-of-the-century marked the period in which winemaking became a fully recognized industry in Sonoma County. Just as the industry began to expand, the growers and vintners were confronted by the threat of temperance which soon cast a dark shadow on their ambitions. With the start of Prohibition in 1920, many of the growers were initially satisfied by the income from grapes sold to eastern markets for non-alcoholic grape juice. Unfortunately, this prosperity did

Riesling Grape Cluster

not last and many wineries were closed and others remained open to make wine for sacramental and medicinal purposes only.

Following Repeal in 1933, Sonoma County and other areas in the state experienced record grape harvests. Although many wineries quickly began to produce and sell their wine to national bottlers, many smaller, family-owned and operated businesses found that it was not as easy to market their wines as prior to Prohibition.

After World War II, as the wine market again suffered from over-production, the number of Sonoma County wineries began to wane and by 1950 the list of active producing wineries was at a record low.

By the mid-sixties conditions had improved and Americans were consuming more wine than ever before. The demand for table wines caused growers to replace their old vineyards planted with Muscat, Burger, Zinfandel and other grapes with premium varietals such as Cabernet Sauvignon, Pinot Noir, Pinot Chardonnay and Johannisberg Riesling. Old wineries were revitalized and new wineries were constructed. Large corporations and private individuals from other professions often got into the wine business without much expertise, but with the naive belief such was the quick and easy way to fame and fortune.

The story of wine in Mendocino County dates back to the original inhabitants of the tree-studded, stream-fed wilderness area, the artistically talented Pomo Indians. The group known as the northern Pomo Indians occupied the present wine region called the Anderson Valley while the group known s the Central Pomo Indians lived in the modern-day wine region of Ukiah Valley.

By 1836, under the Mexican land grant system Rafael Garcia became one of the first Mexicans to own land in the region. He tried his skill at raising livestock and ventured into agriculture. Three years later, another Mexican, Fernando Feliz, followed in his footsteps. Today these two men are chiefly remembered throughout the county because of the two estuaries which bear their names.

As the first adventurous pioneers journeyed north from Napa and Sonoma in the 1840's and in the 1850's, they were attracted by talk of gold in an area at the northern end of the Ukiah Valley. When no gold was to be found, the pioneers settled in the interior valleys, where they harvested lumber, raised livestock, grew grapes, grain fruit and hops. Although the fruits and vegetables flourished, the farmers were faced with the difficulty of establishing an outside market. The only method of transportation were horse-drawn carts.

In the late 1850's commercial grape growing became a popular and in some instances, a profitable business venture. Much of the activity centered around the northern end of the Ukiah Valley.

In 1857, Samuel Orr, a native of Kentucky, was one of the first wine pioneers to bring grape cuttings to Mendocino County. With his wife, Urith, he planted orchards and vineyards 12 miles north of Ukiah in Reeves Canyon. Soon after, Anson Jebidiah Seward, a sometime gold seeker, purchased grape cuttings from Orr and started a vineyard on the same site as the present day Fetzer Vineyards. And, in 1858, Berry Wright

Mount St. Helena

planted grapes in Redwood Valley, north of Ukiah. After several difficult years of trying to raise grapes and sell them commercially, he sold his property.

In 1927 Adolph Parducci purchased a piece of property which he fondly named the Home Ranch. There he happened to find an old vineyard which dated back to the 1880's. It was planted in grape varieties such as Petite Sirah, Carignane, Zinfandel and Alicante. In the thirties, a large group of Italians came to the Ukiah Valley and started family operated wineries. The Ukiah Valley continued to produce wine in a bulk capacity until the increased interest in wine which originated in the middle sixties.

Meanwhile, wine activity was taking place in another wine area, the Anderson Valley. First cultivated in 1851 by settler Walter Anderson, the valley was flourishing with grapevines lacing the hillsides by the 1880's. As the original inhabitants soon learned, the area seemed more suitable for apple orchards than vineyards. However, in the early 1900's, Italian Swiss Agricultural Colony tried to grow grapes in Booneville, a town in the Anderson Valley, but these efforts were unsuccessful. The wine interest of the late sixties and early seventies brought two new wineries to the area, Husch Vineyards and Edmeades Vineyards, and they have had better success, perhaps as a result of more modern technology.

By 1859, Ukiah had become an important center of commerce in Mendocino. That year, it was made the county seat and its administrators organized the county government.

As an alternative to commercial grape growing, many of the Mendocino grape growers decided to build their own wineries and make wine. In 1879, Prussian immigrant Louis Finne and his sons established the first winery in Mendocino County. Situated on a 147-acre parcel north of the town of Calpella, it produced a passable wine from a few acres of Thompson Seedless grapes. By 1914, Finne had expanded his vineyard to include a total of 50 acres. Producing 7,000 gallons a year, he shipped his wine to other areas of California and to markets in the East Coast. The Finne Winery was located on Uva Rd., which means grapes in Spanish.

By 1880, Mendocino County had 330 acres of grapes. Nine years later the railroad was completed between San Francisco and Ukiah and new markets began to open up in wine counties such as Napa and Sonoma. Almost simultaneously, the Old Redwood Highway was under construction.

From 1890 until Prohibition in 1918, individuals and groups of people from countries around the world settled in the Ukiah Valley and started vineyards and wineries. In 1906, George Massoletti built a handsome winery near the town of Calpella and made wine from his 125 acres of Zinfandel vines. In 1915, a group of Finns, who formed the Finnish Colony, planted a large vineyard near the Redwood Valley. And, in that same year, a commune of Scots bought property from Thomas Orr, son of Samuel Orr, and started a vineyard.

During Prohibition, growers continued to raise grapes for commercial markets on the East Coast. A few wineries made altar wines. With Repeal, old wineries resumed their winemaking activities and new wineries were constructed.

onoma County has been an exciting and beautiful land since time began. The dramatic contrast of rugged coast and expansive plains, towering mountains and fertile valleys has been attracting wayfarers for hundreds of years.

The Indians, Pomo, Miwok and Wappo, lived here for thousands of years in virtual paradise. The weather was mild, the streams full with fish, there was plenty of game and the land abounded in roots, seeds and acorns. The word Sonoma is derived from the Suisun language, and translates "vale of many moons."

Much of California's early history was made in Sonoma. It was in turn Indian land, home of the Suisuns and Soto Yomes; a mission settlement; a pueblo; a presidio and northern outpost on which seven different flags were flown--Spain, England, Russia, Mexican Empire, Mexican Republic, California Republic and finally the stars and stripes of the United States.

The last of twenty-one missions was founded here by Fra. Jose Altimira who blessed the spot on July 4, 1823. A chapel was completed the following year and 1000 vines were planted.

Sonoma Valley is considered "the birthplace of California viniculture." Here, ten years after the padres planted their vines, Don Mariano Guadalupe Vallejo set out vines other than the mission variety in 1834.

Harazthy, "the father of California viticulture," imported 100,000 grape cuttings of 140 varieties and became head of the Buena Vista Vinicultural Society, in possession of 5,100 acres of land, 362,000 grapevines and six mountainside cellars, each 125 feet long.

By 1975, Sonoma County produced more wine, by far, than any other county in California. Harazthy's favorite zinfandel vine was the most widely planted grape variety in California by 1900.

Sonoma Valley resident Jack London romanticized Sonoma in his novel "The Valley of the Moon," and spread the work about this unique and beautiful spot. In 1961 the United States government issued the proclamation designating the historic buildings and grounds of the Sonoma Plaza area as a national monument.

Today the Sonoma Plaza is a visitors headquarters where people enjoy picnics, meet friends and delight in the huge shade trees perched on the expansive lawn. Many people enjoy the historic buildings including the restored Toscano Hotel, the barracks (now being restored), Spanish and Mexican adobes, Mission San Francisco de Solano, and the Vasquez house, built by Col. Joseph Hooker which can be admired across the street near the complex of small shops.

The many unique restaurants facing the Square offer elegance in dining and support the claim that the finest wine growing areas of the world also possess the most superior cuisine. Good wine and good food go hand-in-hand here.

The Valley also offers guests the delightful towns of Boyes Hot Springs, Fetters Hot Springs, Glen Ellen, Agua Caliente and Kenwood. This favored recreational region has a championship 18-hole golf course, many swimming pools, riding trails, football and baseball fields, tennis courts, state parks and of course the historic wineries.

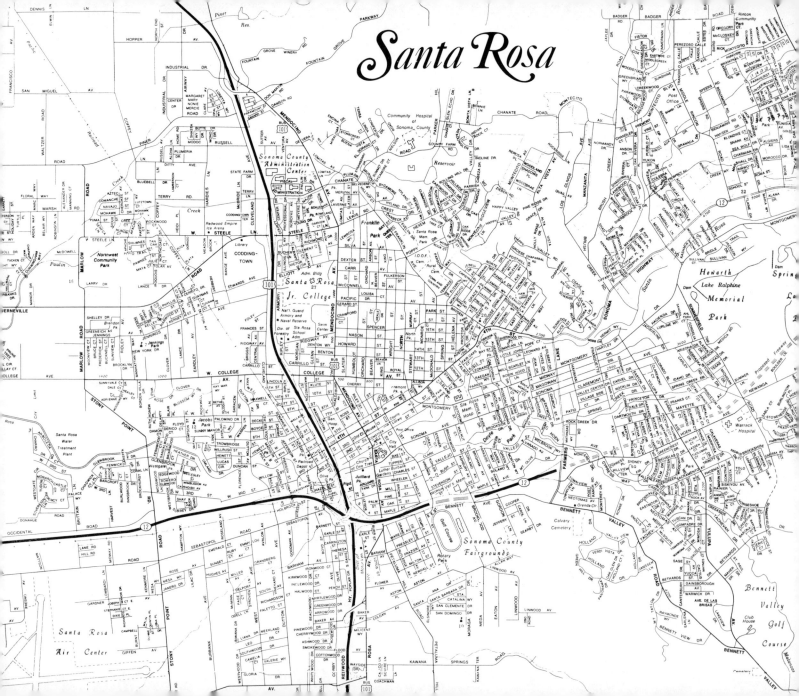

Santa Rosa

ather Juan Amoroso founded the mission of San Rafael and then traveled north to give the beautiful name of Santa Rosa to an area he toured in 1829. While baptizing a young Indian woman in a stream, during his expedition, hostile Indians attacked and forced the priest and his companion Jose Cantua to hurriedly mount their horses and escape. This happened on the day the church celebrates the Feast of St. Rosa of Lima, said to be the only canonized woman saint of the new world. Consequently Father Amoroso named the stream from the incident, the stream named the Valley, and throughout the years this town of Santa Rosa has grown and attracted many colorful residents.

General Mariano Guadalupe Vallejo was sent by the Mexican government to Santa Rosa in 1833. He arranged for Rancho Cabeza de Santa Rosa to be founded by his mother-in-law Senora Carillo, and became the first permanent settlement in the valley.

The Bear Flag Revolt in 1846 brought American settlers and a trading post to Santa Rosa, and the county seat followed in 1854 when Old Peg Leg Menefee stole the court house records in Sonoma and after a wild buckboard ride behind a team of horses, delivered them to the town fathers of Santa Rosa.

Luther Burbank remains one of the most lustrous citizens of Santa Rosa. His home and gardens are now a national monument and this world famous horticultural scientist described Santa Rosa, best of all…"I firmly believe from all that I have seen that this is the chosen spot of all the Earth as far as nature in concerned. The climate is perfect… The air so sweet that it is a pleasure to drink it in… The sunshine so pure and soft; the mountains which gird the Valley are lovely. The Valley is covered with majestic oaks placed as no human hand could arrange them for beauty… Great rose trees climb over the houses, loaded with every color of blossoms… I almost have to cry for joy when I look at the lovely panorama from the hillside." (1875).

Santa Rosa was badly damaged during the 1906 earthquake. The town was rebuilt and thanks to resident Frank P. Doyle, "Father of the Golden Gate Bridge," the town became more closely linked to San Francisco in 1937.

Today Santa Rosa, named "The City Designed For Living," is the largest city in Sonoma County with a population of 66,400 as of January 1, 1976.

Its 26½ square miles contain Robert L. Ripley's world famous church of one tree, golf courses, numerous swimming facilities, tennis, theaters, parks, one of the west's largest shopping centers, excellent hotels, motels and restaurants.

Santa Rosa is the gateway to the Redwood Empire. Located 47 miles north of the Golden Gate Bridge, 100 miles west of Sacramento, 446 miles north of Los Angeles and 21 miles from the Pacific Ocean. The town is surrounded by beautiful vineyards and orchards and has been described as the fastest growing area in the San Francisco Bay region.

Healdsburg

he town of Healdsburg is part of the Sotoyome grant originally made by the Mexican government to Captain Henry Fitch. The romantic episode linked with his name is one of the great legends of the area.

The young American sailor first arrived in California in 1826, soon to be captured by the charms of Josefa Carrillo, daughter of Joaquin Carrillo of San Diego. She in turn was enthralled by the dashing young man. In 1827 he gave her promise of marriage in writing, but because Fitch was a foreigner there were legal impediments. Josefa's parents approved of their plans and a Dominican friar was willing to perform the ceremony. With the utmost secrecy Captain Fitch was baptized on April 14, 1829, at a chapel in San Diego. The friar had promised to marry the couple the following day at the home of the Carrillos, but after last minute preparations, Domingo Carrillo, Josefa's uncle, refused to serve as witness and the ceremony could not proceed. The friar lost his courage despite the arguments, pleadings and tears of the young couple. All he could do was suggest to Fitch that there were other countries with less stringent laws.

Young Josefa coyly suggested that she be carried off by her husband-to-be. He approved the scheme as did her cousin, Pio Pico, even though her parents were not consulted. The very next evening Pio Pico took his cousin up on his horse with him and rode swiftly to a spot on the shore where a boat was waiting. The lovers were reunited on board ship and were married July 3, 1829, at Valparaiso.

The first white settler of Healdsburg township was Cyrus Alexander, a native of Pennsylvania. He had come to California in 1837 and at San Diego made the acquaintance of Captain Fitch, then a prominent merchant. Fitch sent Alexander north in search of land. In the valley of the Russian River he found a fertile tract meeting all the desired qualifications. Fitch made application to the Mexican authorities for the Sotoyome grant of eleven leagues of land, and there Alexander guarded his stock for four years. His payment was one-half the increase plus two leagues of the grant. The land he selected, now called the Alexander Valley, is one of the principal grape growing regions of the Healdsburg area.

It was not until 1852 that Harmon Heald of Ohio located the site of the city. He erected a small cabin to the side of the main road traveling north and opened the first store. He was soon joined by other settlers and by 1857 the name Healdsburg was officially adopted.

Besides the large number of wineries in the immediate Healdsburg vicinity there are several attractions to the town. The annual Prune Blossom Tour through nearby valleys takes place in March and the Russian River Wine Fest is held on the second Saturday in May in the plaza.

Fitch Mountain, so named after Captain Fitch, is a former resort area within one mile of downtown. The uncanny Geysers, located 1700 feet above sea level in the Mayacamas range, produce springs with healing properties long known to the Indians. Picnic facilities are located at Healdsburg Memorial Beach, the Alexander Valley Bridge Campground, and several local wineries.

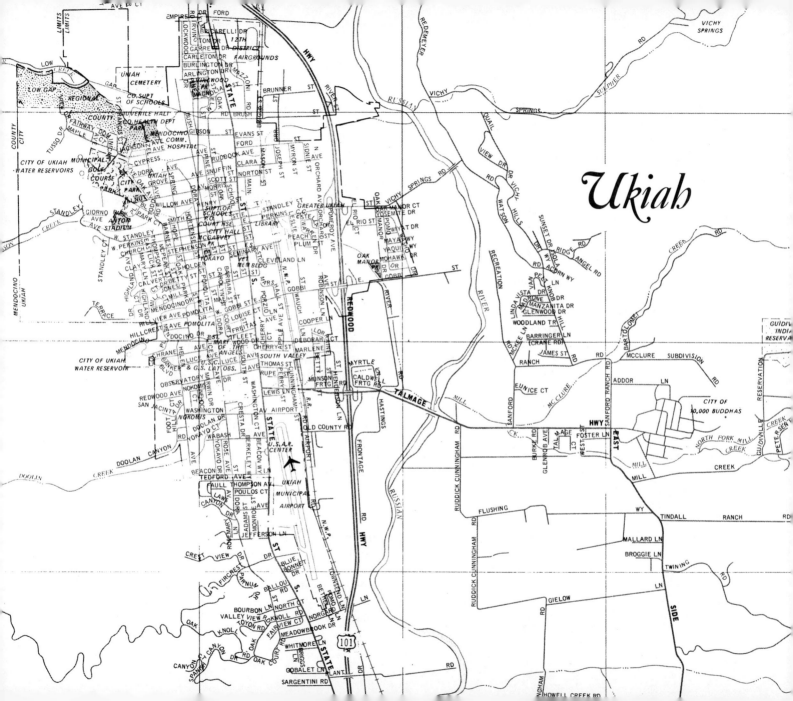

Ukiah

A n independent peaceful group of the Pomos, living apart from the rest of the Central Pomo Indians, existed comfortably in the Ukiah valley for many years. The abundant supplies of fish and wildlife allowed them freedom from tilling the soil. Their first interruption came in 1835 when Captain Sepulvedo Vallejo entered Mendocino County with his troops to capture Indians for work on the buildings in the town of Sonoma.

The first white man in the Ukiah valley was John Parker who arrived as an employee of James Black, a large land owner and cattle rancher of Marin County. For his sake alone, the valley was for some time referred to as the Parker valley. The other name, Yokayo, comes from the Indian wor, Yokaia, meaning south valley.

Of the two Spanish land grants covering Mendocino County, the Yokayo Grant was considered the more important. It had been given to Cayetano Juarez Pio Pico, the governor of upper California in 1845. At. that time the grant covered all of Ukiah valley and the present city of Ukiah. The first settlers were impressed with the beauty of the valley, surrounded by dominant mountains, well-timbered, and bisected by the Russian River. In addition, grass was abundant for the grazing of cattle and sheep, and the soil on the valley floor was found to be particularly productive.

Those settlers who remained and contributed to the growth and development of the Ukiah area arrived between 1856 and 1857. In their search for livelihoods the planting and harvesting of grain became popular immediately due to the mild climate and fertile soil. With popularity came surplus, and grain plantings soon gave way to pears, peaches, tobacco, grapes, and hops. Again, the Pomo Indians furnished much of the labor inharvesting and processing the hops which supplanted tobacco as the major crop of the area. Spotted throughout Sonoma and Mendocino counties old hop kilns or modern buildings modeled after hop kilns are often visible along the roadside.

Grapes were first planted in the Ukiah valley in 1863, about the same time as tobacco. Originally grapes were planted purely for local consumption and because the rocky soil on the hills surrounding the valley floor was found to be suitable for grape vines. Many of the early settlers of the valley hailed from the grape regions of Italy, and both commerical grape growing and home wine production caught on as family business ventures. The first winery in Mendocino County was founded by a Prussian immigrant, Louis Finne, in 1879. By 1880, 330 acres of grapes were thriving throughout the county.

By the year 1859, Ukiah had become the prominent commerce center of Mendocino and as such was selected the county seat. Organization of government, fire department, and railroad as well as construction of bank buildings and residences was underway. Many restored landmark homes predating 1905 today line the streets of residential districts.

The large industrial plant in the Ukiah area is that of Masonite Corporation, a producer of pressed hardboard. Ten miles outside of town is the popular recreation area of Lake Mendocino.

Mendocino

he name "Mendocino" was first applied to Cape Mendocino in 1542 by Juan Rodriguez Cabrillo in honor of Antonio de Mendoza, then the first viceroy of Spain. The area now known as the town of Mendocino was for many years inhabited by the Pomo Indians who referred to it as "Booldam."

The first known white settler was William Kasten, reportedly the sole survivor of a shipwreck off the coast in 1850. He erected a small log cabin near the bluff and lived comfortably among the Indians until he was discovered in 1852 by a scouting party looking for the remains and treasures of a grounded ship from the Orient.

The redwood forests and the adaptability of the area to logging were discovered at the same time, and a company made up of Henry Meiggs, Edward C. Williams, William H. Kelly, J.E. Carlson, and David F. Lansing set sail from San Francisco almost immediately. Another partner, Jerome B. Ford, made the trip overland with the necessary livestock. When the party arrived in July, 1852, they constructed a mill out on the point at the northwest edge of the bay.

Mendocino grew and flourished as a lumber and fishing town despite the problems the initiators had with creditors and with numerous disasters to vessels off the coast. The worst of these was recorded on Nov. 20, 1865, when ten ships crashed into the harbor. Nonetheless, trade did prosper and the population of Mendocino rose to 700. It was not until around 1937 that the market dropped and the mill was in need of much repair. These factors necessitated its closing and for many years the town was at a standstill.

Today Mendocino is reminiscent of Carmel many years ago, primarily in the picturesque ocean setting and the large artist population. Unique to Mendocino, however, is the abundance of 19th century New England-style architecture, all within such a small area. Practically every building in town, whether a business or residence, remains from the time of Meiggs, Ford, Lansing and company.

Since the time of the closing of the mill and the influx of artisans, active restoration of the historical buildings has been in full swing. Particularly noteworthy are the Presbyterian Church, built in 1868 entirely of native redwood, and the Joshua Grindle House, originally the Mendocino Bank of Commerce. Many other historical buildings are easily visible as Mendocino is a town which thrives in part on the charm of its past.

Ten miles north of Mendocino, the town of Fort Bragg serves as headquarters for the "Super Skunk" train. The line runs forty miles between Fort Bragg and Willits along a most scenic redwood route, taking in the Noyo River, wildflowers and apple orchards. A round-trip excursion from either Fort Bragg or Willits takes about eight hours.

Closeby are several of Mendocino County's state parks. MacKerricher State Park is three miles north of Fort Bragg and offers the best camping facilities in the area. Russian Gulch State Park, located between Fort Bragg and Mendocino offers views of the coast and the back country. The main attraction is a blowhole where waves crash against a headland and spout spray high into the air. Van Damme State Park is known for its verdant Sword Fern Canyon as well as its outstanding Pygmy Forest.

Food

isitors to the charming rural areas of Sonoma and Mendocino counties have an opportunity to discover numerous quaint eateries tucked away in the vineyards and redwoods. It is common knowledge, particularly among wine enthusiasts, that wine and food form a most successful and pleasurable marriage. What better way to enjoy the product of the area's sun-kissed vines than to pamper one's palate with accompanying nourishment!

This guide provides a listing of good restaurants for the hungry wine traveler. The area covered, centering around the wineries of the two counties, has a broad range; therefore, the most noteworthy establishments have been included.

The initial list of restaurants to be reviewed in this guide was compiled from the recommendations of winery personnel. The establishments were then evaluated for freshness and quality of food, atmosphere, price range, and service. The following information is intended to inform the reader of what to expect in these categories when visiting the restaurants, rather than to classify or grade them.

For those wishing to picnic, a listing of delicatessens, wine shops, and other unique shops supplying provisions is included. The Sonoma County Farm Trails map, available at local Chambers of Commerce and most winery tasting rooms, lists member farmers, processors, craftsmen, and their outlets. The detailed map locates farms which sell everything from fresh fruit to live Christmas trees. Several picnic areas and campgrounds are also marked.

AU RELAIS   *Restaurant*

As one of the most respected French restaurants north of San Francisco, Au Relais presents aesthetic as well as culinary appeal. The Art Nouveau decor throughout the interior is created by prints on the walls, stained glass, and wood craftsmanship. Outdoor dining is available on the brick patio, surrounded by well-tended flowers and shrubbery.

Owner and chef, Harry Marsden, offers a lengthy luncheon menu of soup, sandwiches, salads, omelettes, crepes, and hot entrees. The House Special Crepe, served with cream sauce and tomato, contains veal, spinach, mushrooms, and cheese.

The dinner menu features a dozen entrees served with soup, salad, garnish, French bread, and coffee or a la carte for $1.00 less. The choice is varied and includes such delicacies as Veal Scallops in cream and Dijon mustard, Roast Duckling cooked with apples or olives, and Cassoulet Maison - a casserole with pork, lamb, beans, sausage, and duck.

The list of desserts is extensive and mouthwatering. Included are French pastries, Brie cheese, and a pastry souffle with apricot sauce.

The thirteen page wine list presents not only wines from most of the Sonoma area wineries, large and small, but also a large collection from Europe.

Au Relais, 691 Broadway, Sonoma 95476. Telephone (707) 996-1031. Hours: 11 a.m.-10 p.m. Mon., Wed.-Fri.; 12 noon-10 p.m. Sat. & Sun.; closed Tues. Price range: Lunch $3.00-$8.00; Dinner $8.00-$12.00. Cards: BA, MC. Seating 100 inside, 50 outside. Full Bar.

BON VOYAGE *Restaurant*

The food reflects the care and interest of this friendly establishment and the hand-printed dinner menu includes Truite aux Amandes ($5.75), Veau des Pechers (veal, spinach and seafood, $8.50), Tournedos Bon Voyage ($7.75) as well as assorted quiches and crepes. All dinners are served with soup, salad and homemade bread.

Omelettes, quiche, sandwiches and crepes grace the lunch menu along with specials like Green Chili and Sour Cream Omelettes and Crepes Ratatouille.

Owners Bill Caraher and Jim Beehler are proud of their extensive local wine list including ZD, Hanzell, and Hacienda Cellars.

Bon Voyage, 23999 Arnold Drive, Sonoma 95476. Telephone (707) 938-3314. Hours: Lunch 10:30 a.m.-2:30 p.m.; Dinner 5:30 p.m.-9 p.m.. Closed Tuesday. Price range: Lunch $.85-$3.25; Dinner $4.50-$8.50. Cards: BA, MC. Seating 125. Reservations accepted.

CAPRI *Restaurant*

Max and Inge Stauffer's dining room on the corner of the Plaza is small and tastefully outfitted with caned chairs, antique reproductions and gorgeous stained glass.

The food is excellent! Luncheon specials include Linguini Vongole (fresh noodles with baby clams and white wine), Manacotti Capri (crepes with veal, chicken and spinach topped with teleme cheese), and Fettuccini Alfredo. Dinner specials of fish and veal are accompanied with a special appetizer, soup, green salad, French bread and sweet butter. Sunday Brunch is served with a champagne cocktail, fresh fruit goblet, coffee and corn bread with honey.

Capri Restaurant, 101 East Napa St., Sonoma 95476. Telephone (707) 996-3866. Hours: Lunch 11 a.m.-3 p.m.; dinner 5 p.m.-10 p.m.. Price Range: Lunch $2.50-$4.25; Dinner $5.50-$9.50. No Liquor. Wine list varied, $5.00 corkage fee. Cards: BA, MC. Seating 42.

DEPOT HOTEL 1870 *Restaurant*

The Depot Hotel is a gastronomic oasis set on a quiet side street several blocks from Sonoma's historic town square. The outstanding dining experience at the Depot Hotel is complimented by the comfortable and refined ambiance of this landmark structure which was originally built in 1870 and was once owned by General Vallejo. On balmy summer evenings intimate candle-lit tables may be reserved around the outdoor pool.

The "Chef's Choice" menu offers three or four exquisitely prepared entrees each served with hors d'oeuvres, delightful soup du jour, crisp green salad and homemade dessert, and the veal and chicken dishes are of particular note.

The wine list offers several good vintages from Sonoma Valley wineries and Korbel champagne is available by the glass.

Owners Russel Brown and William Griffin invite guests to view the cozy kitchen facilities on an apres dinner tour.

One note of warning: the Depot Hotel enjoys a reputation of excellence and consequent popularity; weekend dining can sometimes be rather hectic.

Depot Hotel 1870, 241 1st. West, Sonoma. Telephone (707) 938-2980. Hours: Thurs.-Sun. 5 p.m.-9:30 p.m. (no dinner on 1st Sun. of the month); Fri. lunch 11:30 a.m.-2 p.m.; Brunch 11 a.m.-2 p.m. (1st Sun. of month only.) Price range: Brunch $6.00; Lunch $5.00; Dinner $9.50. Cards: BA, MC, AE. Seating capacity: 95. Corkage $2.00. Wine only.

GINO'S OF SONOMA *Restaurant, Bar*

After a stroll around Sonoma's historic plaza, the friendly atmosphere of Gino's provides a relaxing stopover for lunch or liquid refreshment. Proprietor Jerry Rosenberg has renovated the building yet maintained some of the historic flavor.

Lunch, which is served daily from 11 a.m. to 4 p.m., offers sandwiches, salads, and steaks. The lavish Shrimp and Crab Louies are served with hard-boiled egg, beets, kidney beans, avocado, peppers, tomato, cucumber, and olives. The generous half-pound hamburger ($2.50) comes with appropriate garnishes.

Gino's of Sonoma, 420 First St. East, Sonoma 95476. Telephone (707) 996-2636. Hours: 11 a.m.-1 a.m. Price range: Lunch $2.50-$5.75. Cards: BA, MC. Seating 50.

SONOMA FRENCH BAKERY *Provisions*

The Sonoma French Bakery is a shrine for genuine Sourdough French Bread lovers. This is absolutely the finest French bread found.

Lili and Gratieu Guerra are quick to reveal their "secret ingredient" which is dedication, willingness to work hard, and concern for how the bread turns out.

The Guerra's moved to Sonoma from France in the mid-1950's. They feel their bread is as good or better than any in France.

Sonoma French Bakery, 468 1st St. East, Sonoma 95476. Telephone (707) 996-2691. Hours: Wed.-Sat. 8 a.m.-6 p.m.; Sun. 8 a.m.-12 noon. French bread 65¢; also pastries, cookies, and decorated cakes.

SONOMA CHEESE FACTORY   *Provisions*

Celso Viviani, the patriarch of this cheese factory, arrived in Sonoma during 1912. He was employed by the Sonoma Mission Creamery in the early 1920's and was finally able to open his own plant with a partner in 1931. The newly-renovated Cheese Factory has been serving cheese, wine and delicatessen items since 1945. The Cheese Factory offers outdoor cafe dining, wine-- tasting by the glass or taste, their famous Sonoma Jack, sandwiches to order and catering in true wine country style.

The Sonoma Cheese Factory, 2 W. Spain St., Sonoma 95476. Telephone (707) 996-2300, 996-JACK. Hours: 9 a.m.-6 p.m. daily. Cards: BA, MC, AE. Seating 25 inside, 75 outdoor garden.

SWISS HOTEL   *Restaurant*

The Swiss Hotel dates back more than 140 years to the time when it was owned by Captain Salvador Vallejo. The present owners, Ted and Helen Dunlap, are proud to state, "The Swiss Hotel has been in the same family for 53 years." Although the Hotel operates on a very limited basis, the restaurant is known for its home-cooked Chinese and Italian dinners prepared by Fred Wing for the past 39 years.

Swiss Hotel, 18 West Spain St., Sonoma. Telephone (707) 996-9822. Hours: Dinner 5 p.m.-9:30 p.m. Wed.-Sat.; 2 p.m.-8:30 p.m. Sun.. Price range: Complete Chinese Dinner $5.25, Italian $3.85-$7.25. Lobster $11.00. Cards: MC. Seating 65.

VELLA CHEESE CO.   *Cheese Factory*

The Vella Cheese Company is very much a part of picturesque Sonoma and visitors still drive up to the old stone and wood factory to purchase their hand-made cheese. Everyone knows a good thing, so one can expect a wait in line to buy their cheese.

Young Joe Vella came to San Francisco from his native Italy in 1916. He sold butter, eggs and cheese, learned the business and his family has been providing excellent cheese at bargain prices for Sonoma county residents since 1931.

The cheese sells from $1.35 to $1.95 per pound. It is weighed and packaged when purchased.

Vella Cheese Co., 315 2nd. St., East Sonoma. Telephone (707) 938-3232. Hours: 9 a.m.-5:30 p.m.; closed Sunday. No Cards.

THE GLEN ELLEN INN   *Restaurant*

Robert Franks and his wife Kai opened their charming restaurant two years ago in the small town of Glen Ellen.

They have successfully applied their non-commercial approach to food preparation by orienting their customers to the craft of good cooking. They are devotees to the axiom that "the eye eats first". Every carefully prepared dish is not only a pleasure to eat but a delight to look at.

The menu includes 15 different omelettes, considered by Mr. Franks to be his specialty. The dinner menu offers a choice of 2 entrees which vary daily. Their Sunday brunch is a unique experience in this part of the valley. Specialties include Eggs Benedict, Eggs Florentine and Chicken Liver Omelettes. Another feature of the house is the excellent coffee, the Franks' own blend.

Selected wines from Sonoma and Napa counties are available.

The moment you enter this well-ordered restaurant you realize the owners pay attention to all details. The food is well prepared, the service excellent and the ambiance is tidy, simple elegance.

Glen Ellen Inn, 13670 Arnold Drive, Glen Ellen 95442. Telephone (707) 996-9906. Hours: Lunch 10:30 a.m.-3 p.m., Dinner 5 p.m.-8 p.m., Wed.-Sat.; Special Sunday Brunch 10:30 a.m.-3 p.m.. Price range: Lunch $1.60-$2.85; Dinner $4.50-$7.00. No cards. Seating 28. Reservations recommended.

LONDON GLEN VILLAGE   *Restaurant, Provisions*

General Vallejo built this grist mill in the late 1840's and the Chauvet family purchased the historically unique building several years later. A stone winery (once the largest in the Valley of the Moon), was opened on the property in 1881, and continued producing wine and brandy until 1967.

Today we find a rich variety of restored buildings, skilled artists and fine craftsmen nestled in this historic Mill and Wine Village.

The gourmet restaurant, shops, galleries, fine arts, wine and food combine to recreate the spirit of an earlier time. The Grist Mill Inn serves all of one's favorite sandwiches for lunch as well as omelettes, breakfasts and soup & salad with Sonoma French bread. The dinner menu includes homemade soup and salad bar, fresh vegetable, potato or rice, Sonoma French bread and ice cream. Abalone steaks and fresh broiled salmon predominate the menu. There is also a chef's special on the weekends.

The London Glen coordinator, Ellen Baughman, adds, "Our intention is to use the Village to perpetuate the historic values of the area. There's a lot of exciting history in this place and we want to bring it to life again for everyone to enjoy."

London Glen Mill & Wine Village, 14301 Arnold Drive, Glen Ellen 95442. Telephone (707) 938-1616. Open daily from April-January. Hours: 11 a.m.-2 a.m.. Price range: Lunch $1.25-$3.75; Dinner $3.00-$8.25; Sunday Brunch $3.75. Cards: BA, MC. Reservations suggested.

MOOSETTA'S *Take-out Provisions*

Located just south of Fiesta Market on Sonoma Highway in Boyes Hot Springs is a small shopping complex that houses Moosetta's.

This unassuming pastry and entree business has been delighting piroshki lovers for 15 years with their cabbage, meat or all-vegetable assortment enclosed in dough and made fresh daily.

Visitors are greeted with a smile and the wonderful odors coming from the tidy and homey kitchen, where Marv and Caroline Joyce hand make all the assorted pastry and fillings for their varied menu.

Moosetta's Pastries and Entrees, 18808 Sonoma Hwy., Boyes Hot Springs 95416. Telephone (707) 996-1313. Hours: 10 a.m.-6 p.m. Wed.-Sat.. Price range: $.85-$3.50. Take-out food, no seating.

THE BELVEDERE *Restaurant, Cabaret*

The Belvedere has been a Historical Landmark in Santa Rosa since the turn of the century. The mansion houses a restaurant, unique specialty shops and galleries, and is a fine example of Queen Anne Style architecture, combining grace, elegance and simplicity.

Owner, investor Leonard Shelley and John Duran have extensively restored this building and created a place "where the past meets the present for your enjoyment today."

The lunch, brunch, dinner and dessert menu is printed all-in-one and features international and vegetarian cuisine. Sandwiches, salads, crepes, and creative platters from which you may prepare your own or nibble are offered for lunch. The "Dinner-in-a-Salad" is half an avocado stuffed with mandarin chicken and garnished with almonds and vegetables, all on a bed of lettuce. The chef prepares a vegetarian dinner special daily as well as all the breads and pastries. Complete dinners are served with soup du jour, house salad, and a basket of freshly baked rolls.

The restaurant and cabaret boasts live entertainment nightly, presenting local performers as well as world-famous artists. The selection of wine is small but intriguing.

The Belvedere, 727 Mendocino Ave., Santa Rosa. Telephone (707) 542-1890. Hours: Lunch 11 a.m.-2:30 p.m. weekdays; Brunch 10:30 a.m.-2:30 p.m. Sat. & Sun.; Dinner 5:30 p.m.-10 p.m. Tues.-Sun.. Price range: Lunch $2.50-$4.25; Brunch $2.95-$4.95; Dinner $4.95-$8.95. Cards: BA, MC. Seating 99. Full bar.

FIORI, GRACE, & CO. PUB CAFE   *Restaurant, Bar*

The second generation of the well-known local families of Fiori and Grace have combined their knowledge and talents to launch this "Pub Cafe". Italian and American dinners are offered in convivial surroundings. Remodeling improvements to the building include skylights, booths with etched glass partitions and low hanging lamps, antiques, and stained glass.

The ten seafood dishes are the most recommended from the extensive dinner menu. Eighteen entrees feature steaks, veal, and chicken; and fourteen pasta plates are primarily spaghetti dishes with a choice of sauces. Complete dinners include Mama Fiori's Original Minestrone soup, a tossed green salad, vegetable, and a choice between potato, rice, spaghetti or ravioli.

The luncheon menu offers omelettes, salads, sandwiches and pasta.

Behind the swinging door is the contemporary "Pub" where a one-man show of music and comedy invites audience participation on Thursdays, Fridays, and Saturdays beginning at 9:30 p.m.. The remaining nights of the week, tables are pulled back and a jukebox provides the music for those who wish to dance.

The carefully selected wine list offers wines at $1.00 above retail and has enough diversity to please most palates.

Fiori, Grace & Co., 2755 Mendocino Ave., Santa Rosa 95401. Telephone (707) 527-7460. Hours: Lunch 11:30 a.m.-3 p.m.; Dinner 5 p.m.-11 p.m.. Price range: Lunch $1.85-$5.95; Dinner $4.95-$12.50. Cards: BA, MC, AE. Full Bar. Seating capacity: 150.

HILLTOPPER   *Restaurant, Bar & Grill*

At the top of a natural landscaped driveway off Montgomery Drive in Santa Rosa is found the newly remodeled HillTopper.

General manager Stu Betz has utilized his years of restaurant and wine experience into "an uncommonly casual place with surprises."

The lunch menu features Charmaine London's crepes ($2.95-$3.40), Fighting Joe Hooker's Hamburgers ($2.75-$3.40), Old Adobe Salad Corner ($.95-$4.25), Soup and Sandwich Platter ($1.75-$2.65), and Peg Leg Menefee's Belly Busters ($3.25-$4.50).

Dinner specials include Coquille St. Jacques ($7.25 shrimp, crab and scallops baked in supreme sauce), Teriyaki Top Sirloin ($6.95, marinated and broiled to perfection), and Veal Oscar ($6.60, sliced sauteed veal topped with crab meat and asparagus, served with HillTopper rice). The restaurant offers a nice view of the surrounding Sonoma hills and Lake Ralphine. There is dancing and live music five nights a week.

A very intelligent and comprehensive wine list features sixteen wineries, large and small, all sold at about $1.50 above retail prices. Happy Hour, from 4:30-7 p.m. Monday through Friday, features drinks two for the price of one; wine at $.75 a glass, mixed drinks at $1.10, plus free hors d'oeuvres.

HillTopper, 3901 Montgomery Blvd., Santa Rosa. Telephone (707) 528-7755. Open seven days. No lunch Sat., Sun. and Mon. Price range: Dinner $4.95-$9.25; Lunch $1.75-$4.25. Cards: BA, MC. Seating 100. Reservations suggested.

MANDALA CAFE — *Vegetarian Restaurant*

This is the place to come to treat yourself to pure, healthful, vegetarian food. The menu is interesting and inexpensive; the service pleasant and friendly.

Michael Hirschberg and his involved staff are responsible for the well-known success of the Mandala and are quick to invite all questions concerning the origin or preparation of any of their special items including the fresh homemade soup, bagels and bread, as well as the daily $2.35 luncheon special.

Any doubts of the healthful quality of their food are forgotten as one leaves the Mandala Cafe. Above the door is a sign "Eat here and die old."

Mandala Cafe, 620 Fifth Street, Santa Rosa 95404. Telephone (707) 527-9797. Open Mon.-Sat. Hours: Lunch 11 a.m.-3:30 p.m.; Dinner 5 p.m.-9 p.m.. Price range: Lunch $.95-$2.85; Dinner $1.95-$4.25. Live music every night. No cards. Seating 50.

MARK WEST LODGE — *Restaurant Francais*

The Mark West Lodge is majestically perched above Santa Rosa on the road to Calistoga and is considered the oldest resort (since 1833) in existence in California today.

Host, Rene Pavel, is the guiding light of this establishment and sets the stage for dramatic dining in his Rene Room which sports a waterfall, elegant surroundings, attentive waiters and the excitement of many flaming dishes.

His refined menu offers eight entrees including Mark West tossed salad, fresh vegetable and potato. They are: La Coq a la Phesant ($8.95, breast of chicken with fine spices, wine and pate de foie); Roast Port Loin a l'Orange Sauce ($8.95); Canard a la Mark West ($9.95, roast duckling aux orange flambe); Van Gouste Grille Beurre Fondue ($15.00, broiled lobster tail); Kavkasky Shasslik on flaming sword ($9.95, marinated lamb with onion, bacon, green pepper served with rice pilaf); Mark West Steak ($11.00, the finest sirloin strip steak); Carre d'Agneau a la Rene ($24.00 for two, roast rack of lamb); and Roast Prime Ribs of Beef ($9.95).

Many French wines are found on the wine list as well as some fine local wines.

Mark West Lodge, 2520 Mark West Springs Rd., Santa Rosa. Telephone (707) 546-2592. Hours: Cocktail lounge 5-10 p.m. daily, 2-9 p.m. Sun.; Dining room 5:30-10 p.m. daily, 4-9 p.m. Sun.. Closed Wed.. Open Mar. 1 to Thanksgiving. Cards: MC, BA, AE. Seating 110. Reservations recommended.

OLD MEXICO   *Mexican Restaurant*

Forget about every Mexican restaurant you have dined at and turn yourself over to the experience of authentic family recipes of Old Mexico.

The visitor is met at the reception area, guided among ferns, murals and gorgeous tiles, then seated in either an elegant booth or an ornately-carved chair.

Fresh warm chips and an interesting hot sauce reflect the wish of owner Tony Lopez to provide the ultimate in Mexican cuisine.

The menu is expensive and exciting. Their Tostada de Gallina ($1.95) is a meal itself with chicken, avocado strips and sour cream served hot and sumptuous with lettuce, tomato, tortilla and sauce. The enchilades ($3.95-$4.95) are deliciously served with choice of soup or salad, corn tortillas y mantequilla, coffee and dessert. Steak, lobster and prawns are available ($4.95-$10.95) as well as sampler platters ($4.95) with enchilada de Res, chile relleno, taco de Res, arroz, frijoles, tortillas, mantequilla and cafe.

Old Mexico is a must for Mexican food fans. There is a fine quality here found nowhere else.

The full bar offers fantastic Margueritas, Mexican and American beers and a few wines including Chenin Blanc from Santo Tomas, Mexico.

Old Mexico, 4501 Montgomery Drive at Mission Blvd., Santa Rosa. Telephone (707) 539-2599. Hours: 11 a.m. -10 p.m. Sun.-Thur.; 11 a.m.-11 p.m. Fri. & Sat.. Price range: $1.95-$10.95. Cards: MC, BA, DC, CB. Seating 150. Banquet facilities and food-to-go. Full Bar.

THE PAINTED HOUSE — *Restaurant*

The Painted House is just that - a lovely old Santa Rosa house that has been tastefully converted to a restaurant which local artists have made into a visual experience.

The lunch menu is headed with "Soups, Salads, and..."; an amazing array of pleasing dishes. Soup ($.70-$1.00), salad ($1.00), quiche and salad ($2.75), sandwiches ($1.95) include cream cheese with avocado and sprouts, turkey, ham, salami, and roast beef. The Painted House palettes, an artful array of cold delicacies ($2.95-$4.95) features a cheese board and meat board with fresh fruit. The "Hot off the Easel" choices ($2.50-$3.75) include crepes, seafood, Mexicana, canneloni, le Parisien and welsh rarebit.

The dinner menu includes soup and salad and features Canard a la Maison ($6.75, crisp roast duckling with orange and prune sauce), Veau Wellington ($7.75, milk fed veal baked in pastry with Madiera sauce), and Pork a l'Orange ($6.25, lean roast loin of pork with orange and Grand Marnier sauce).

The wine list is well thought out and fairly priced about $1.00 above retail including numerous bottles from small local wineries.

The Painted House, 721 College Avenue, Santa Rosa. Telephone (707) 527-7537. Hours: Lunch, 11 a.m.-3 p.m. Mon.-Fri.; Midday Soup & Salad 3 p.m.-5:30 p.m.; Dinner 5:30 p.m.-10:30 p.m. Mon.-Sat.. Price Range: Lunch $1.75-$3.95; Soup, Salad, & French bread, $2.25; Dinner $5.50-$8.25; Corkage $2. Cards: MC, BA. Seating 60. Reservations suggested.

TRAVERSO'S DELI — *Provisions*

Since 1933, the Traverso family has been providing Santa Rosa residents with a fantastic array of gourmet foods, cheese, wine, liquor and Italian cold cuts.

The present building, beautifully constructed, was given a civic award for its architecture and has still retained the image of the "Deli that smells good."

The wine selection is the best in Santa Rosa and includes domestic as well as imported liquors and cordials. Steve Lorenzen heads the wine department with much knowledge and enthusiasm.

Traverso's, Corner of 3rd and B Sts., Santa Rosa. Telephone (707) 542-2530. Hours: Daily 8 a.m.-6 p.m. Closed Sundays.

WINE CAVE — *Provisions*

Chuck Chapman started his liquor center 12 years ago and has since added the Delicatessen and Wine Cave with its impressive California Wine selection. Ninety-five percent of the wineries in California are said to be represented here as well as a good supply of imports and liquor.

His international Deli serves sandwiches ($1.49) and salads ($.35), pastries, chicken and ravioli and for people in a hurry, a phone call ahead will provide the "Fastest Lunch in the West" upon arrival.

Wine Cave, 2255 Cleveland, Santa Rosa. Telephone (707) 525-9463. Hours: Deli, 7 a.m.-7 p.m. daily, 10 a.m.-6 p.m. Sat. & Sun.; Liquor, 10 a.m.-12 p.m. daily, 10 a.m.-1 a.m. Fri. & Sat.. Cards: MC, BA.Seating 45.

CHATEAU MARGOT   *Restaurant*

Marjorie and Joseph Salas have owned and operated French restaurants in the Bay area for thirty-five years. Beginning with Chez Joseph and Marjorie, every one has been listed as one of the best restaurants in northern California. Their success might be attributed to Joseph's meticulous preparation and presentation of food, but Marjorie puts equal care into the minute details of the decor, the service, and the wine list.

Chateau Margot, their most recent venture, promises to be one of the most popular gourmet restaurants in Sonoma County. After spending six months renovating a dilapidated Victorian house, they decorated it as they thought it might have been. The effect is one of charm and elegance. For intimate dining, try to reserve one of the two secluded tables - one is set in a circular bay window, the other in the remodeled maid's bathroom.

Dining at Chateau Margot is truly a gourmet experience. There are ten entrees, ranging from veal in a cream sauce to Lobster Thermidor, blended in a white wine sauce. Each entree is preceded by soup, salad, spinach crepes, and a "petite entree".

Marjorie's wine list offers an excellent selection of imported wines and champagnes. The California representation is limited by comparison.

Chateau Margot, 876 Gravenstein Hwy. S., Sebastopol 95472. Telephone (707) 823-5720. Hours: Wed.-Sat. 6 p.m.-9:30 p.m., Sun. 5 p.m.-8:30 p.m.. Price range: $7.25-$10.25. No cards. Corkage $2.50. Reservations suggested. Seating capacity: 42.

GIOVANNI'S DELICATESSEN   *Provisions, Deli*

For those on the way to the coast from Sebastopol, Giovanni's is a natural stop for picnic provisions. The selection of meats and cheeses is standard delicatessen fare, and all sandwiches are made to order.

For such a small location owners John and Judy Filippa and John Failing have used their space very efficiently to offer additional delicacies such as pasta, artichoke or zucchini frittate and homemade desserts.

A very good selection of domestic and imported beer is offered, but the most time and effort has obviously been put into the wine selection.

Giovanni's Delicatessen & Wine Shop, 171 Pleasant Ave. North, Sebastopol 95472. Telephone (707) 823-1331. Hours: 8:00 a.m.-7:00 p.m. Monday-Saturday; 10:00 a.m.-5:00 p.m. Sunday. Cards: BA, MC. Seating 15 plus outdoor patio.

LE POMMIER   *Restaurant*

Jean Pierre Saulnier, the warm-hearted chef and proprietor of this French country-style establishment, is to be complimented not only on his cuisine but also on his reasonable prices. Le Pommier has long been a favorite of Sebastopol residents, and since words of praise have spread, Jean Pierre has expanded his facilities. The atmosphere remains informal and hospitable, and the decor is simple because the emphasis here is on enjoyment of the meal.

Dinner entrees are presented simply and include soup, salad or steamed artichoke, vegetable and coffee. The soups are delightfully authentic and flavorful, whether French onion or cream style. The salads of lettuce garnished with cucumbers, tomatoes, carrots and mildly spiced chicken are dressed with a unique, piquant house dressing that is distinctive in its herb subtleties.

Item number one on the menu and specialty of the house is the fish of the day, always delectable as it is caught fresh and prepared specially according to the chef's whim. Other entrees include Chicken Saute with white wine, tomatoes, onions, and sweet peppers; scallops sauteed in garlic and lemon; Veal Cordon Bleu; and several steaks, most of which are accompanied by a delicate sauce.

Le Pommier, 1015 Gravenstein Hwy. South, Sebastopol 95472. Telephone (707) 823-9865. Hours: Dinner 5:00 p.m.-9:30 p.m. daily; Lunch 11:30 a.m.-2:00 p.m. Tuesday-Saturday. Price range: Dinner $5.50-$11.00; Lunch $2.75-$6.50. Corkage: $2.75. Cards: BA, MC, AE. Seating capacity: 92.

THE TOWN'S DELI & RESTAURANT *Provisions, Deli*

After over thirty-five years in the restaurant business, El Smits, with the help of his wife and family, has opened an exceptionally fresh and modern deli in the heart of downtown Sebastopol. The menu offers thirty combination sandwiches, including five vegetarian, and any one may be ordered hot. Portions of high quality meats and cheeses are generous and reasonably priced.

Other features include El's homemade Quiche Lorraine with salad ($1.75), a good choice of healthful salads, barbequed chicken, and homemade desserts.

The Town's Deli & Restaurant, 6970 McKinley, Sebastopol 95472. Telephone (707) 823-1822. Hours: 9:30 a.m.-6:30 p.m. Monday-Friday; 9:30 a.m.-6:00 p.m. Saturday. No cards. Seating capacity: 42.

L'OMELETTE   *Restaurant*

Leon Arseguel began his gourmet cooking career when he was a boy and has been preparing French meals for fifty-two years. After retiring once, he and his wife, Antoinette, opened this intimate cafe in the center of Forestville.

Complete dinners, including soup, salad, potato, vegetable and coffee, are very reasonably priced. Specialty entrees include Breast of Capon Monte Carlo, Tournedos Filet of Beef, and Coquille of Sea Food Riviera, a combination of shrimp, scallops and mushrooms in cream sauce.

L'Omelette, 6685 Front St., Forestville 95436. Telephone (707) 887-9945. Hours: 5:30 p.m.-9 p.m. Fri.-Sun. only. Price range: $4.00-$8.75. No cards, no checks. Seating capacity: 30.

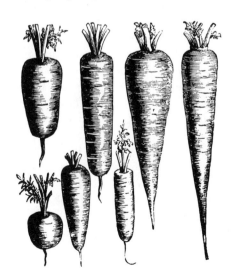

RUSSIAN RIVER VINEYARDS   *Restaurant*

Just below the redwood and concrete winery building designed by Robert Lasden in 1969 is an old shingled house where new owners, the Chan family, operate the restaurant as well as the tasting and sales room.

Extremely popular is the Sunday Brunch, especially attractive in suitable weather because of the seating on the outdoor brick patio which is beautifully landscaped. Tables are semi-sheltered by shade trees and the natural atmosphere is very often complemented by the soft music of a live guitar. The impressive hop kiln styled towers of the winery add a dramatic note to the scenery.

Brunch may be purely fruit and croissants served with sweet butter and jam, or a lavish display of champagne, a fruit melange, and a choice of meticulously prepared Eggs Benedict, French toast, or vegetable quiche.

The dinner menu changes at least every other week, offering specialties from around the world and emphasizing wine sauces. There are usually four choices, covering seafood, poultry and meat dish categories.

The wine list features imported wines with a few Napa additions and ranges in price per bottle from $3.50 to $30.00.

Russian River Vineyards, Hwy. 116, 5700 Gravenstein Hwy. South, Forestville 95436. Telephone (707) 887-1562. Hours: Thurs.-Sun. dinner 6 p.m.-10 p.m.; Sunday brunch 11 a.m.-2 p.m.. Price range: Dinner $7.00-$10.00; Brunch $2.95-$5.95. Cards: BA, MC. Reservations advised. Seating 100.

HEXAGON HOUSE
Resort

Just outside the entrance to the Armstrong Redwoods State Park, the strikingly modern Hexagon House offers a restful and refreshing retreat in an informal atmosphere.

Accommodations include both motel-style rooms and eighteen individual cottages. All are attractively furnished in modern decor and some have their own kitchens. Each cottage offers its guests the utmost privacy, nestled back among the trees and on the border of a springlike meadow.

The restaurant was originally designed as the studio of an art school, but the distinctive architecture has lent itself well to being transformed into a rustic dining room and a charming tropical cocktail lounge with ferns, windows, and view. There are a number of unusual paintings and furnishings from a private collection to complete the decor.

The chef specializes in Prime Ribs of Beef au Jus, offered daily, but there are a number of daily specials including Manchurian Chicken, Veal Oscar, Mongolian Beef, and several fish entrees. Also available daily are the standard steaks, lamb chops, and chicken.

Hexagon House, 16881 Armstrong Woods Road, Guerneville 95446. Telephone (707) 869-3993. Rates: Motel $24.00-$28.00, Cottages $28.00-$33.00 for two people. Off season rates 30% less. Restaurant hours: 6 p.m.-10 p.m. daily; also 10 a.m.-2 p.m. Sunday Brunch. Price range: Dinner $6.25-$12.50; Brunch $3.50-$4.65. Coffee Shop hours: 8:30 a.m.-4 p.m.. Cards: BA, MC, AE, DC. Full bar. 38 Units.

THE TIDES
Restaurant, Motel, Fishing Party Boats

The picturesque harbor of Bodega Bay was discovered 200 years ago and named in honor of Don Juan Francisco De La Bodega y Caudra. It has remained a seafood center and since the 1930's the pioneer fishing families of Antonio and Zankica have offered this "all-in-one-stop" on the coast that is open all year. Along with the restaurant, modern motel and gift shop, The Tides wharf has sport fishing boats, marine fuel, bait and tackle, liquors off-sale, ice, and Union 76 products.

The busy season starts on April 1st, and a two-week advance notice is recommended at the motel. Doubles start at $16.80 and two-bedroom cottages with kitchen start at $30.00 per day.

The fishing boats leave The Tides wharf promptly at 7 a.m. daily and return about 2:30 p.m.. Individual rates start at $14.00 per day for bottom fishing and $17.00 per day for salmon trolling. A deposit is required on all reservations.

The restaurant offers an abundance of fresh fish on its menu: oysters on the half shell, lobster tails, scallops and swordfish steak all seem to taste better while viewing the ocean from your table. The Tides has a full bar and features Charles Krug and Sebastiani Vineyards on their wine list.

The Tides, P.O. Box 186 on Coast Hwy 1, Bodega Bay 94923. Telephone (707) 875-3553. Hours: Daily 5:30 a.m.-10 p.m.. Price range: Breakfast $.65-$2.60; Lunch $1.45-$4.95; Dinner $4.95-$12.50. Cards: BA, MC. Reservations recommended.

THE SALAME TREE DELI   *Restaurant, Provisions*

The Salame Tree Deli is more than a deli. It is also a self-service restaurant and a natural and gourmet foods store, housed under the Italian flag with the Salame Tree emblem. The menu on the wall offers the traditional meat and cheese combinations as well as a wide variety of homemade items. Chef and manager Jim Wilmarth prepares daily all of the salads, three to four soups, his own spaghetti and ravioli, and desserts including carrot cake and walnut pie.

The Salame Tree Deli, 304 Center St., Healdsburg 95448. Telephone (707) 433-7224. Hours: Monday-Friday 8 a.m.-8 p.m.; Saturday-Sunday 10 a.m.-6 p.m.. No cards. Seating capacity: 54.

COSTEAUX FRENCH BAKERY   *Provisions*

The red and white striped awning hanging in front marks this bakery a block and a half north of the Plaza in downtown Healdsburg. Now in his fifth year at this location, Jean Costeaux began his baking career in France, spent six years at the Sonoma French Bakery, and now he and his wife, Annie, own and operate their own business.

Costeaux is perhaps best known for his croissants and authentic French bread, varying in loaf size from baby and baguette to pound-and-a-half.

Costeaux French Bakery, 421 Healdsburg Ave., Healdsburg 95448. Telephone (707) 433-1913. Hours: Wednesday-Saturday 8 a.m.-6 p.m.; Sunday 7:30 a.m.-12:30 p.m.. No cards. No seating.

TAMAULIPECO   *Restaurant*

Jose Ramirez, who has worked in restaurants almost all his life, was inspired to open his own by his mother's cooking, who helped him in preparing the meals in the first days of the business. Today Jose's wife, Celia, does all the cooking with Jose's help. His mother's recipes still inspire them, particularly for their month-long specials (watch for the small white tag clipped to the menu).

The most popular of these specials is the Jumbo Shrimp Tostado with beans, lettuce, guacamole, anchovie sauce and shrimp on a whole wheat tortilla. The $2.00 for lunch and $3.00 for dinner include beverage and dessert. The regular menu offers a variety of a la carte items, priced separately for lunch and dinner, as well as ten different combination plates priced $2.40 to $3.25. In addition, six authentic Mexican dinners such as Chile Verde and Bistec Asado are available. Each meal at Tamaulipeco begins with a small plate of tortilla chips surrounding a bowl of hot(!) sauce specially prepared by Jose.

The atmosphere, too, is authentic, maintained by the handpainted murals and ceremonial skirts on the walls, the music on the jukebox and the selection of four Mexican beers. The wine list is extremely limited but Sangria is offered.

Tamaulipeco, Cnr. Adeline & Ward, Healdsburg 95448. Telephone (707) 433-5202. Hours: 11 a.m.-9 p.m., closed Mon.. Price range: Dinner $.70-$4.95; Lunch $.50-$3.25. Cards: BA, MC. Seating 40.

DRY CREEK LIQUORS   *Provisions*

Proprietor Kevin O'Conner is not only a wine and liquor merchant, but also a Dry Creek valley vineyard owner and dedicated home winemaker. His appreciation for wines dates back to his college days in Rome, Italy, where he first sampled the delights of European wines. An extensive collection of North Coast varietal wines, a representative sampling of wines from the remainder of California, and a small selection of European wines are features that have given this store a fine reputation.

Dry Creek Liquors, 177 Dry Creek Road, Healdsburg 95448. Telephone (707) 433-5529. Hours: 9 a.m.-11 p.m. Sun.-Thurs.; 9 a.m.-12 midnight Fri. & Sat. Cards: BA, MC.

PLAZA DELI   *Provisions, Delicatessen*

Don and Rachel Reed, the friendly proprietors of the Plaza Deli, have used their imaginations to come up with the tasteful combinations in the sandwiches on their menu. Among the favorites are the Dana ($1.50), with roast beef, turkey, cheddar and tomatoes; the Pink Panther ($2.00), made up of lox, Swiss cheese, tomatoes and onions on an onion roll; and the Black Russian ($1.45), consisting of smoked liverwurst, pastrami and jack cheese on black bread.

They also stock imported beer and a wide selection of Sonoma county wines.

Plaza Deli, 109 Plaza St., Healdsburg 95448. Telephone (707) 433-2530. Hours: 9 a.m.-7 p.m. Monday-Saturday. Cards: BA, MC. Seating capacity: 25.

HOFFMAN HOUSE   *Restaurant, Delicatessen*

At the Hoffman House Helen and Mannie Riggs live and operate one of the popular country luncheon stops of northern Sonoma county.

Inside, there is a personal hospitality that emanates right from the kitchen as Helen is always ready to greet the traveler with a bowl of homemade soup, a salad or a specially prepared hot or cold sandwich made up of meat and/or cheese from the deli counter on your choice of bread. Also offered daily are her mushroom quiche ($2.75) and her tamale pie ($3.00), both meals including salad, bread and butter.

The Saturday night dinners (by reservation only) feature a different one of Helen's creations each week, among them Beef Wellington, Cioppino, Rack of Lamb and Chateaubriand. All dinners include a first course of soup or other light dish, fresh vegetable, salad, fruit and cheese, a joyous homemade dessert and coffee.

An entire room is devoted to a display of Sonoma and Mendocino wines available at winery prices, and there is an excellent selection of imported and domestic beer. If you prefer to eat outside, tables are available on the porch or in back under a weeping willow. Picnics are packed upon request.

Hoffman House, 21712 Old Redwood Hwy, Geyserville 95441. Telephone (707) 857-3818. Hours: 11:00 a.m.-5:00 p.m. daily; closed Tuesday November-May. Sunday Brunch 11:00 a.m.-1:00 p.m.. Dinner Saturday night by reservation only. Price range: Dinner $8.75-$9.50, Sunday Brunch $3.25, Lunch $1.25-$3.00. Cards: BA, MC. Seating capacity: 45.

MAMA NINA'S   *Restaurant*

One mile north of Cloverdale on Highway 101 is the original Mama Nina's where Nina Delfino lived and operated her Italian restaurant until 1972.

Now dinners are served in almost every room of Nina's old house including the "bedroom" where the single table seats eight.

Before turning her restaurant completely over to present owner George Wilson, Nina taught him how to make his own pasta, the accompanying sauces, and soup. The pasta is kneaded, rolled and cut daily, and the sweet basil for the delightful pesto sauce is grown outside the kitchen door.

A la carte entrees are served with soup or salad while complete dinners for $1.75 extra include antipasto tray, Nina's minestrone, salad, homemade dessert and beverage. The Tagliarini is especially popular, but for those pasta lovers who have difficulty making a choice, try the mixed pasta plate made up of ravioli and Tagliarini pesto and Caruso.

In addition to pasta, Mama Nina's menu offers Veal Scallopini, Chicken with wine and mushrooms, Abalone, Scampi (prepared with butter, olive oil, garlic and lemon), Lobster, and four different steaks.

The wine list features eight local wineries, priced $1.00 to $1.50 above shelf price.

Mama Nina's, P.O. Box 896, Cloverdale 95425. Telephone (707) 894-2609. Hours: 5:00 p.m.-10:00 p.m. Wednesday-Saturday, 5:00 p.m.-9:00 p.m. Sunday, closed Monday & Tuesday. Price range: $3.95-$12.00. Cards: BA, MC, AE. Seating capacity: 75 inside, 40 outside. Full bar service.

THE GREEN BARN   *Restaurant*

Easy to locate once you are in the south end of Ukiah, the exterior of the building is unmistakably a green barn with white trim. Inside the atmosphere is plain yet pleasant; the menu straightforward and simple. Most of the items listed are available for both lunch and dinner.

The Green Barn is probably most popular among the locals for its Prime Rib ($7.25), although Pacific Salmon ($4.50), Frogs Legs when available ($4.95), fit well within the family budget. All dinners include garlic bread and a choice of salads, potatoes, spaghetti and dessert

The Green Barn, 1190 So. State St., Ukiah 95482. Telephone (707) 462-9995. Hours: 11 a.m.-11:30 p.m. Mon.-Sat; 4 p.m.-10:30 Sun.. Price range: $1.25-$10.50. Cards: BA, MC. Seating 75. Full bar.

CHICK'S HOUSE OF SPIRITS *Provisions, Wine*

The wine selection here is limited, but more comprehensive than any other store in Ukiah. The large underground cellar consists of well-displayed bottles from several of the larger Sonoma and Napa wineries, most of the local Mendocino wineries, and quite a number of imports. Several shelves of wine books are available for reference and sale.

Upstairs amid the liquor, pop wine and party supplies, is a small counter of delicatessen cheeses, meats, and salads, all moderately priced.

Chick's House of Spirits, 290 So. State St., Ukiah 95482. Telephone (707) 462-5663. Hours: 10 a.m.-10 p.m. Monday-Friday; 10 a.m.-11 p.m. Saturday; 10 a.m.-8 p.m. Sunday. Cards: BA,MC.

HENNE'S ICE CREAM *Provisions*

The Henne family maintains the old-fashioned high quality by using fresh cream and other natural ingredients in their ice cream and candies, all of which they produce right there in the shop. Any one of the fifteen to eighteen flavors of ice cream exudes freshness and richness.

Real ice cream enthusiasts will rejoice when they see the prices here. Hand-packed pints go for $.80 and quarts for $1.55.

Henne's Homemade Candies & Ice Cream, 582 No. State St., Ukiah 95482. Telephone (707) 462-5661. Hours: Fall to Spring Sunday-Wednesday 12:30 p.m.-9:00 p.m., Thursday-Saturday 12:30 p.m.-10:00 p.m.; Summer 10:00 a.m.-10:00 p.m. daily. Cards: BA, MC.

HOUSE OF GARNER *Restaurant*

Over the years the House of Garner has remained one of Ukiah's most well-respected family restaurants, serving breakfast, lunch and dinner daily.

The dinner menu is extremely varied, offering traditional Continental and American cuisine with a few interesting twists. Examples are their Coquilles St. Jacques, scallops and shrimp in a light curry sauce; and their Tenderloin of Beef a la Stroganoff, tender pieces of beef in a delightfully herbed sauce over rice. Other entrees range from deep-fried oysters to rack of lamb. Service is excellent, portions are adequate, and the entrees, although not superb, are well-presented and reasonably priced.

The lunch specialty is the "Rib Sticker", an old-fashioned meat and vegetable stew, served with salad, bread and butter. Equally appetizing are four imaginative burger combinations, all served on grilled English muffins.

The wine list is limited and moderately priced.

A unique feature at House of Garner is the Cabaret Dinner Theatre. The plays are performed by the Northern California Performing Arts Center and may be viewed with or without a meal. The standard price of admission is $9.50 with meal, $4.00 without.

House of Garner, 1090 So. State St., Ukiah 95482. Telephone (707) 462-2376. Hours: Breakfast 7 a.m.-12 p.m.; Lunch 12 p.m.-5 p.m.; Dinner 5 p.m.-11 p.m. daily. Price range: Breakfast under $3.50; Lunch $1.25-$4.95; Dinner $4.95-$12.95. Cards: BA, NC, AE, CB, DC. Full bar service.

THE LIDO
Restaurant, Bar

Irv Styer has retained much of the friendly atmosphere originated in 1905 by the founder Simon Casabonne. His interest in wine is apparent both in the decor of the intimate "cellar room", a private dining area seating twenty-eight, and in the featuring of a "Wine of the Month" from one of the Mendocino county wineries on his wine list.

The dinner menu ranges from seafood and steaks to Italian dishes. The specialty is Quail a la Grappa, locally raised quail stuffed with a grape dressing and served with lightly seasoned rice.

The Lido, 228 E. Perkins St., Ukiah 95482. Telephone (707) 462-2212. Hours: Lunch 11:30 a.m.-2:30 p.m. Mon.-Fri.; Dinner 5 p.m.-10:30 p.m. Mon.-Thur., 5 p.m.-11 p.m. Fri. & Sat.. Closed Sun. Price range: Lunch $1.95-$4.25; Dinner $3.65-$14.95. Cards: BA, MC, AE, CB. Reservations advised. Seating 140.

BROILER STEAK HOUSE
Restaurant, Bar

Young Jose Fernandes emigrated from Portugal to learn the restaurant business from his uncle, founder of the Broiler Steak House. Tony Fernandes truly valued the importance of a quality meal and an efficient restaurant, and in order to insure this quality after he inherited the business, Jose still cooks two nights a week in addition to overseeing general management.

As the name suggests the specialty of the house is pit-broiled steak, cooked the "old California way" over oak wood. Among the favorites are the Special Dinner Steak ($5.95), an incredibly tender Broiled Filet Steak ($8.25), and Surf and Turf ($12.50); but a variety of juicy steaks cooked to your taste are available on the menu in addition to barbequed spare ribs and chicken and several seafood choices.

All dinners include soup served with warm rolls, an extremely generous salad of lettuce, fresh vegetables, and garbanzo beans topped with house dressing, and a choice of baked potato or French fries. When seated in the main dining room all preparation is visible. You can watch your steak on the broiler while enjoying your second helping of salad.

The wine list is limited to four Ukiah area wineries and the variable corkage fee is high.

Broiler Steak House, Uva Drive, Redwood Valley 95470. Telephone (707) 485-7301. Hours: 4:00 p.m.-11:00 p.m. Monday-Saturday, 3:00 p.m.-10:00 p.m. Sunday. Price range: $2.25-$12.50. Cards: BA, MC. Seating capacity: 600 (including five banquet rooms). Full bar service and cocktail lounge.

GREGORY'S   *Restaurant*

Gregory Seubert has brought a little bit of old Bavaria to the fishing village of Albion. Tables line the front wall of windows looking out to a superb ocean view from high on a bluff.

The menu represents both the local fishing industry and the heartier dishes of Gregory's homeland. The favorite is Gregory's Pepper Steak ($9.50) for which regulars return to relish time and time again. A unique dish is the German Enchilada ($6.95) consisting of a crepe-style pastry stuffed with spiced crabmeat and covered with a mustard sauce.

———

Gregory's, Highway 1, Albion 95410. Telephone (707) 937-0272. Hours: 5:00 p.m.-10:00 p.m. Wednesday-Sunday; closed January. Price range: $6.95-$10.95. Cards: BA, MC. Reservations recommended. Full bar service. Seating capacity: 50.

PICCADILLY DELI   *Restaurant, Provisions*

Down in the Albion flats amid the fishing boats, Nancy and Paul Puder operate this clean and refreshing delicatessen with a spacious view of the Albion River and its activities.

Sandwiches, salads, crepes, and casseroles are served daily for both lunch and dinner. The kitchen produces one-course home-style meals, nothing elaborate, but good satisfying food. Imported beer, Mendocino wines, and a variety of fruit juices are also available.

The Puders rent canoes at $2.00 per hour for picnics up the river.

———

Piccadilly Deli, Albion River, Schooner's Landing Marina, Albion 95410. Telephone (707) 937-5703. Hours: 10 a.m.-5 p.m. Wed.-Sun.; 6 p.m.-9 p.m. Fri.-Sun.. Closed Dec.-Mar.. Price range: Lunch $1.65-$2.45; Dinner $3.00-$4.00. No cards. Seating 28.

LEDFORD HOUSE   *Restaurant*

Located just four miles south of the town of Mendocino on Highway 1 is the historic Ledford House where owner and chef Barbara Mastin creates not only a mystical and intimate atmosphere but also some of the most distinctive dishes ever tasted. The service is warm and hospitable, in keeping with the timeless decor, and as explained on the menu, if it seems a little slow it is simply because everything is prepared fresh and to order. This gives the diner a chance to relax and enjoy the charms of the ocean view, the fireside and the food.

The menu varies with the season, yet the kitchen produces consistent quality. All dinners consist of homemade brioche rolls and butter served in a chilled scallop shell, a fresh garden salad, mouthwatering homemade soup, entree and fresh vegetable.

The fresh fish of the day is dictated by the local catch. Your waiter describes in detail the type of fish and the method of preparation as well as the chef's specialty of the day, usually a meat dish. The most requested item on the menu is the Shrimp Cannelloni, made up of tiny shrimp, shallots, mushrooms and herbs rolled in extremely tender homemade pasta and baked with sauce and aged cheeses.

The wine list is small but offers a good selection from several of the smaller wineries of Sonoma and Mendocino.

———

Ledford House, Highway 1, Little River 95456. Telephone (707) 937-0282. Hours: Tuesday-Saturday 6 p.m.-10 p.m.. Price range $9.50-$10.95. No cards. Corkage $1.50. Reservations required. Seating 32.

LITTLE RIVER CAFE   *Restaurant*

Tucked away behind the Little River post office, this unique little French cafe is truly authentic, from the prints on the wall to the homemade desserts. Debbie, Jacques, Sylvie and Francois have developed a reputation for outstanding quality in the meals they prepare. The menu varies with the changes in available fresh foodstuffs, but everything is always created from "scratch". Consequently, they have the freedom to elaborate on the classical French styles of cooking and the spontaneity produces many a rare treat.

There are three nightly entrees served with soup, salad and homemade bread, and the owners often do not know until the day before exactly what the entrees will be. The consider their specialty to be lamb, particularly a lamb ragout known as "gigots haricots". Another favorite is Chateaubriand sauce madere. For vegetarians a phone call a day ahead of time is all that is necessary for the chefs to prepare a meatless gourmet meal. In every entree a distinct effort is made to keep the meal light and digestible, yet at the same time satisfying.

In keeping with authenticity, the wine list is entirely French.

———

Little River Cafe, Highway 1, Little River 95456. Telephone (707) 937-0404. Hours: Friday-Monday dinner two seatings at 6:30 p.m. and 8:30 p.m.; Saturday-Sunday brunch 9 a.m.-1 p.m.. Price range: Dinner $7.50-$8.50, Brunch $1.00-$3.00. No cards. Reservations required. Corkage fee: $2. Seating 18.

CAFE BEAUJOLAIS   *Restaurant*

New owners Joel Clark, Karin Cole-Hedspeth, and Margaret Fox are off to a fine beginning. Set in the relaxed country atmosphere of one of Mendocino's older homes, their hospitality reaches out of the pastel-printed wallpaper to the antique oak tables, every one complete with fresh cut flowers.

On Thursdays, Sundays, and Mondays, country-style dinners are served a la carte with the idea of serving a complete meal in one dish for $5.00. Friday's and Saturday's dinner is Table d'hote, complete with homemade bread, sweet butter, soup of the day, salad, rice or potatoes, vegetable and coffee. The entree is cooked French style and varies depending upon local fresh food availabilities.

Breakfasts include a choice of omelettes, waffles, fruit and coffee cakes. Lunches offer omelettes, quiche, soup, fruit salad and sandwiches. The conspicuous freshness of all items is highlighted by the fact that nearly everything is homemade or homegrown.

Joel Clark has put together a most interesting wine list including varieties from Sonoma, Mendocino, and Napa and a good selection of French and German wines.

———

Cafe Beaujolais, 961 East Ukiah St., Mendocino 95460. Telephone (707) 937-5614. Hours: 7:00 a.m.-9:00 p.m. Sunday, Monday, Thursday; 7:00 a.m.-10 p.m. Friday-Saturday. Closed Tuesday and Wednesday. Price range: Breakfast $.50-$4.00, Lunch $.75-$3.00, Dinner $5.00-$11.00. No Cards. Reservations recommended. Corkage fee $1.00. Seating capacity: 40.

THE CHEESE SHOP   *Provisions*

Tom and Barbara Wallerich are very busy people. Somehow, between catering and designing interiors in the Mendocino community, they find time to run their shop. Although they specialize in an extensive offering of imported and domestic cheeses, the remainder of the shop is excellent for browsing and gift shopping.

Barbara travels a great deal, in part to gather merchandise for the store, and the interest in wine is apparent when you enter the "wine cellar". The selection is quite good considering the space allowed and includes many tenths suitable for picnic baskets. The Wallerichs are expecially proud of their selection of French Burgundies. The wine bar is now open for tasting Friday through Monday and is hosted by Tony Wood, the well-respected wine buyer for the Heritage House. These tastings should prove to be educational and beneficial for both tourists and locals. A small selection of imported beer is also available.

Among the eyecatchers are imported baskets, both large and small, an array of linens, glassware, exotic cookware, kitchen utensils, and gourmet delights. One of the unique features is a selection of Marilyn Douglas' Homemade Mendocino Jams & Jellies, every one preserving the fresh whole fruit flavor of locally grown and hand selected fruit. The Cheese Shop is the sole outlet for these old-fashioned preserves.

———

The Cheese Shop, Cnr. Little Lake & Lansing, Mendocino 95460. Telephone (707) 937-0104. Hours: 10 a.m.-6 p.m. daily. Cards: BA.

THE SEAGULL *Restaurant*

After recovering from a disastrous fire in December, 1976, which burned their business to the ground, owners David and Cathy Jones have recently opened the new Seagull. The modern angular architecture distinguishes the structure markedly from the standard New England style which predominates in Mendocino. The use of natural wood grain, house plants, and contemporary stained glass windows provides a relaxed atmosphere in this extravagant coffee shop.

Undeniably the favorite breakfast spot in town, the Seagull offers a complete menu of juices, fruits, cereals, eggs and other familiar favorites. Lunches feature a variety of sandwiches and salads.

The dinner menu is surprisingly varied, specializing in Chicken Kiev and Lamb Persian, the latter served with yoghurt and peaches. Fresh local fish is featured. The a la carte section is lengthy and very reasonably priced, including a bargain soup and salad dinner for two with French bread and wine for $5.45. The wine list is the standard distributor list with a couple of small Mendocino county wineries included.

One of the big attractions to the Seagull is the "Cellarbar" located upstairs from the restaurant. Here comfortable chairs around a large fire pit and before a wall of plate glass windows offer a leisurely setting.

———

The Seagull, cnr. Lansing and Ukiah Sts., Mendocino 95460. Telephone (707) 937-5204. Hours: 8 a.m.-9 p.m.. Price range: Breakfast $.50-$4.25; Lunch $1.25-$4.95; Dinner $3.50-$7.95. No cards. Full bar. Seating 55.

THE RESTAURANT *Restaurant*

A former drug store and pharmacy now houses The Restaurant, owned and managed by Jim and Barbara Larsen and Rose Nunes. The simple decor is enhanced by the intriguing and intimate paintings of local artist Olaf Palm.

The lunch menu offers a number of interesting sandwiches, omelettes, and salads along with a special entree, sandwich and dessert of the day. The entrees range from quiche to exotic Greek dishes. On Sundays an everchanging brunch menu offers such delicacies as Eggs a la Goldenrod, Hangtown Fried Oysters, or waffles served with specially prepared fresh fruit syrups.

Dinners are primarily seafood, one of the favorites being trout stuffed with crabmeat, mushrooms, sherry and green onions. The chicken saute with artichoke hearts, pearl onions and wine is also recommended. All dinners are served with soup and salad or *bagna cauda*, a plate of raw vegetables with a warm dipping sauce made up of olive oil, butter, garlic and anchovy. For the budget conscious a special soup supper for $4.00 is a generous meal of green salad, soup, bread, a glass of wine and fruit and cheese.

The wine list offers hard-to-get wines from several small wineries of the North Coast counties at reasonable prices.

———

The Restaurant, 418 N. Main St., Fort Bragg 95437. Telephone (707) 964-9800. Hours: Lunch 11:30 a.m.-2 p.m.; Dinner 5 p.m.-9 p.m.; Sunday brunch 10:30 a.m.-2 p.m., closed Wednesday. Price range: Lunch $.85-$4.25; Dinner $3.75-$9.50. Cards: BA, MC. Seating 68.

Lodging

ravelers to the regions north of San Francisco Bay have a variety of sights, sounds and smells from which to choose. Viewing the natural beauty of California's mountain ridges pitching to the sea is one of man's favorite pastimes. The coast line stretching along Sonoma and Mendocino Counties is magnificent, whether fog-shrouded or crystal clear. The orchards, meadows and fields of the agricultural region of Sonoma County convey a peaceful reassurance in contrast to the urban centers only a few hours away, while the unspoiled splendor of Mendocino's towering redwood forests remain seemingly invulnerable.

Such appealing attributes have long enchanted visitors to both counties although to complete the picture, visits to the local wineries are essential. There is a mystical, timeless quality in the experience of inhaling the aroma that lingers in the cellars, in viewing the casks and barrels that contain so much wine, and in sampling the product where it is made. After a full day of touring winery facilities and tasting rooms, the visitor may have need of rest.

The following hotels, inns, resorts, and campgrounds have been listed to aid the overnight visitor to the wine country of Sonoma and Mendocino. The variety offered is extensive due largely to the broad area covered, although there are numerous other campgrounds along the Russian River and the coast and scattered among the redwoods in Mendocino County.

Reservations for desired accommodations are advisable during the peak touring months from May to November.

SONOMA HOTEL   *Lodging, Restaurant*

The Sonoma Hotel will take the traveler back through its 100 years of history and acquaint him with the charm of an old world caravansary.

This three-story hotel, located at Spain St. and First St. West, has been recently renovated by owners John and Dorene Musilli. Old time bathtubs in five rooms, lovely old beds, antiques from Europe and California heirlooms are found in each of the 17 beautiful rooms.

The Old Sonoma House Restaurant downstairs provides nightly entertainment at the piano bar. Lunch, dinners and Sunday Brunch featuring the wines of Sonoma county and patio dining (weather permitting). There is a special every Friday night, two complete meat or vegetarian dinners for the price of one. They have chef's special crepes and torts Friday, Saturday and Sunday, and also serve what can be considered the biggest and best hamburgers in the valley. The other dinner choices include Vegetarian Quiche ($5.50), Veal Parmesan ($6.50), Seafood Plate (in season $6.50), Chicken in White Sauce ($5.95), Old Sonoma House Salad ($4.95) and New York steaks cut to the size of your appetite (6 oz. $6.75 to 12 oz. $9.95).

Sonoma Hotel, cnr. Spain St. & First St. West, Sonoma. Telephone (707) 996-5103. Lodging rates: $28.00-$45.00 with continental breakfast. Restaurant hours: Lunch & Dinner 11 a.m.-10 p.m.; Sunday Brunch 9 a.m.-3 p.m.. Price range: Lunch $1.95-$3.50; Dinner $4.95-$6.50; Sun. Brunch $3.95 with champagne.

JACK LONDON STATE PARK   *State Park*

Jack London State Historic Park, a small portion of London's original 1,500-acre Beauty Ranch was acquired by the State of California in 1959, partly through a gift from Irving Shepard (London's nephew and an heir to the London estate).

Along with the natural beauty of the landscape, the main features of the park include the House of Happy Walls, the ruins of the Wolf House and Jack London's grave site.

There is no overnight camping and no formal picnic facilities are available. All visitors are requested to observe the opening and closing hours: 10 a.m.-5 p.m..

Jack London State Historic Park, P.O. Box 358, Glen Ellen 95442. Telephone (707) 938-5216.

LONDON LODGE   *Restaurant, Lodging*

Bill and Marie Colling have owned the rustic London Lodge Restaurant in Glen Ellen for the past ten years; their consistently good food and dining location above beautiful Sonoma Creek delights guests and promotes their friendly family atmosphere.

Their proficient daughter Pamela does all of the cooking at the restaurant. Her specialties include Beef Stroganoff ($4.95-$6.25), Beef Brochettes($5.25-$6.50), Saute Sweet Breads ($6.50) and Stuffed Filet of Sole ($8.50). Their steaks and seafood are favored for their regular customers and are available in weight watchers portions.

Monday night is Spaghetti night. $3.50 buys a large plate of delicious spaghetti with green salad and hot garlic French bread. Another feature is the Champagne Dinner for Two ($11.50) including a choice small steak or fried chicken and a split of champagne or house wine.

There is a full bar with a very interesting collection of owls and offers special before- and after-dinner cocktails.

Newly added is the 22-unit motel next door with a kidney shaped pool and plenty of free parking. Rooms start at $25.00. The complex is located at the foot hill entrance of Jack London State Park.

London Lodge, 13740 Arnold Drive, Glen Ellen 95442. Telephone (707) 996-6306. Hours: 4 p.m.-11 p.m. Fri.-Sat.; 4 p.m.-10 p.m. Mon., Thur., & Sun.. Cards: BA, MC, DC, AE. Seating 97. Banquet room for 200. Full bar.

SONOMA MISSION INN *Lodging*

This is the Grand Old Hotel of the Wine Country in the Valley of the Moon. The Inn is an hour's drive from San Francisco. It offers comfortable, charming relaxation and good food in an informal atmosphere.

Whether swimming in the pool, lounging in the sunshine, playing shuffleboard, ping pong, or enjoying the quiet of the tree-studded lawns, this Inn captures some of the grandure of the past with its huge ball-room, lobby and acres of tended gardens.

Sonoma Mission Inn, P.O. Box 1, Boyes Hot Springs 95416. Telephone (707) 996-1041. Hours: Breakfast, 7:30 a.m.-9 a.m.; Dinner, 5 p.m.-6 p.m.. Room Rates: Single $16.00-$19.00; Double $16.00-$19.00; Queen & King Beds $20.00-$26.00; Family Rooms $18.00-$20.00. Small, well-mannered pets are welcome.

SUGARLOAF RIDGE STATE PARK *Campgrounds*

The park is open all year and offers camping, riding and hiking on 25 miles of trails on this 2,000-acre site. There are 50 campsites, each with tables and benches, charcoal barbeque stove with grill, level tent sites and parking spur. No reservations are accepted. There are no picnic facilities.

The park is located midway between Sonoma and Santa Rosa. Turn on to Adobe Canyon Road from Hwy 12 near Kenwood and proceed three miles to the entrance. The roads are narrow and steep.

SugarLoaf Ridge State Park, 2605 Adobe Canyon Road, Kenwood 95457. Telephone (707) 833-5712. Camping $2.00 per night. Picnic $1.50. Dogs $1.00 each with rabies certificate.

LOS ROBLES LODGE   *Restaurant, Lodging*

Claus Neumann, energetic President of the Corporation at Los Robles, has over the years developed a reputation for fine food preparation and wine knowledge.

The restaurant at Los Robles Lodge is elegant and offers a full continental and western menu. Daily specials (Mon.-Thurs.) $5.50. Fridays: Neptune's Festival Buffet $7.50. Saturdays: Roast Duckling Montorency $6.50. Sundays: Roast Leg of Lamb $5.50.

Your choice of 21 dinner entrees include their special hors d'oeuvres cart, choice of soup du jour or salad and vegetable, potatoes or rice, bread and butter. The local favorites are the Medallion of Beef Bernaise ($8.00), Sauteed Abalone steak ($9.00), and Chateaubriand Bouquetiere for 2 ($21.00). Lunch and dinner can be accompanied by a bottle of wine from the Claus Vineyard in Healdsburg, (the Gamay Beaujolais is excellent), or a choice from a comprehensive list of other Sonoma County Wines.

The Lodge offers 90 rooms, all equipped with king, queen or two double beds, air conditioning, color cable T.V., free movies, radios, coffee, free parking and telephones. Two swimming pools are available to guests.

Los Robles Lodge, 925 Edwards Ave., Santa Rosa. Telephone (707) 545-6330. Restaurant Hours: Lunch 11:30 a.m.-2:30 p.m. daily; Dinner 5 p.m.-10 p.m.; Sunday Brunch 10 a.m.-2 p.m.. Price range: Lunch $2.40-$5.00; Dinner $5.50-$12.00; Corkage $1.50. Lodging prices start at $21.00 per night. Cards: MC, BA, CB, AE, DC. Seating 120.

SHERATON TROPICANA   *Lodging*

The Sheraton Tropicana, described as the Palm Springs of Northern California, is the largest motor Hotel and Convention Center in the area. Three hundred deluxe rooms and apartments are arranged on 25 acres of lawn and palms.

Arrangements can be made for groups of ten to two thousand in their twenty meeting rooms or 20,000-square-foot Convention Center.

Other features include a hot therapy pool, 3 full-size swimming pools, cocktail lounge, coffee shop (open 24 hours), Steak Ranch Dining Room, rock music 7 nights a week and dancing.

The Sheraton Tropicana Steak Ranch offers Sebastiani and Korbel wines from $2.50 to $6.50. The dinner menu is split between the Tropicana Steak Ranch offerings and the Tropicana Delux Dinners. Both include the delightful salad smorgasbord, choice of soup or salad, and baked Idaho russet or whipped potatoes on the delux dinners. Salad specialties are also on the dinner menu ($2.65-$4.95).

Sheraton Tropicana, 2200 Santa Rosa Ave., Santa Rosa 95401. Telephone (707) 542-3655. Rates: Lodging summer rates Twin or Double 1 person $22.75, 2 persons $28.75; winter rates twin or double 1 person $20.75, 2 persons $26.75. Restaurant price range: Breakfast (served around the clock) $1.50-$4.45; Lunch $2.15-$4.95; Dinner Steak Ranch $5.95-$9.95, Tropicana Delux Dinners $5.65-$7.25. Cards: BA, MC, AE, CB, DC, VISA.

SANDMAN MOTEL   *Lodging*

The Sandman is one of the newest motels in the Santa Rosa area. It is easily found by taking the Mendocino Avenue exit on Hwy 101 north of Santa Rosa.

There is a 24-hour restaurant across the street. 112 rooms with showers and tubs, a heated pool, sauna, color T.V., air conditioning, and a conference room. Pets allowed.

Sandman Motel, 3421 Cleveland Ave., Santa Rosa 95401. Telephone (707) 544-8570. Rates: 1 person $19.00; 2 people $22.00; Room with 2 double beds $24.00. Cards: MC, BA, AE, DC.

FARMHOUSE LODGING   *Inn*

Cousins Ivan Kobelansky and Steven Palavanchi had a desire to open a restaurant in an older Sonoma County house. After many months of searching they located a well-worn 1890's Victorian farmhouse set right on Russian River Road just outside of Forestville. The more recent cabins which had been built for weekly rental units forced restaurant plans out of the immediate picture and the two owners set about remodeling for lodging purposes.

Within the house itself are three double-bedded rooms and one bathroom. The additional building encloses two studios and four two-room units, each with a kitchen, bathroom, and one double bed. Three of these units are capable of handling four people. Each room has a personality of its own after being furnished with antiques and plants, and all units with the exception of those rooms in the house are available at weekly rates.

Attractions to Farmhouse Lodging are the swimming pool, badminton court, and fifteen acres with spring, waterfall, and redwoods. For those passers-by not wishing to brave the Russian River but desiring a swim before moving on to the next winery, the charge is $3.00 for the use of the pool.

Farmhouse Lodging, 7871 River Road, Forestville 95436. Telephone (707) 887-1623. Rates: Rooms in house: Single $9.00, Double $12.00; Studio units: Single $17.00-$23.00, Double $20.00-$25.00; $3.00 for each additional person. Weekly rates equivalent to five times daily rate. Cards: BA, MC. Reservations recommended. Number of units 9.

CAZANOMA LODGE   *Resort*

Under the new ownership of Randy and Gretchen Neuman, the idyllic Cazanoma Lodge continues in the peaceful tradition of the past thirty years.

Although only two cabins are available presently, the Neumans have plans to open three bedrooms on the second story of the lodge next year. According to schedule, a few "winterized" cabins with fireplaces will be completed soon after.

The main floor houses a restaurant where German and American dinners are served. Both dining room and bar overlook a scenic waterfall and trout pond.

Cazanoma Lodge, P.O. Box 37, Cazadero 95421. Telephone (707) 632-5255. Open Wed.-Sun, May-Sept.; Fri.-Sun. only Mar., Apr., Oct., Nov.. Rates: $16.00-$20.00. Restaurant hours: 5 p.m.-10 p.m. weekdays, noon-10 p.m. Sat. & Sun.. Price range: $5.50-$10.25. Cards: BA, MC. Reservations advised. Units: 2.

LU-ANN MOTEL
Motel

The Lu-Ann Motel, a member of the Friendship Inns of America, is located one mile north of Ukiah's downtown business district and within one block of Highway 101. Deluxe modern accommodations are immaculately clean and offer color cable T.V., stereo music, and individually controlled heat and air conditioning.

Special features include queen-size beds with extra length, waterbeds, a heated swimming pool and sauna.

Lu-Ann Motel, 1340 No. State St., Ukiah 95482. Telephone (707) 462-8873. Rates: Single $14.00-$20.00, double $24.00-$26.00, $2.00 each additional person; kitchens $28.00 minimum. Reservations recommended. Cards: BA, MC, AE, CB, DC. Number of rooms 72.

MOTEL SIX
Motel

Of the seventy locations throughout California, Ukiah's Motel Six is basically no different from the rest. There are one or two motels in the area with lower rates but you will sacrifice the cleanliness and some of the comforts of Motel Six. Here sixty-four well-kept units offer in addition to beds: baths, air conditioning, swimming pool privileges, and easy access to downtown Ukiah.

Motel Six, 1208 So. State St., Ukiah 95482. Telephone (707) 462-8763. Rates: Single $8.95, double $10.95. Television: $.50/day. No personal checks or credit cards. Reservations suggested. 64 rooms.

THE MANOR INN
Motel, Restaurant

The Manor Inn is one of Ukiah's most attractive modern motels within walking distance of downtown. Every room is clean and comfortable, and each is newly carpeted and furnished. Standard features for all units are silent heat and air conditioning, color cable T.V., and direct dial phones.

Next to the pool is the dining room and cocktail lounge where the chef's partiality to seafood is evidenced by the offering of Chef's Neptune Seafood Platter consisting of scallops, prawns, oysters, codfish, crab and salmon served with two sauces and French fries, a bargain at $7.75.

Manor Inn, 950 No. State St., Ukiah 95482. Telephone (707) 462-7584. Rates: Single $14.00-$18.00, Double $18.00-$22.00. Restaurant hours: 7 a.m.-10 p.m. daily. Price range: Breakfast $1.25-$4.25; Lunch $1.50-$4.25; Dinner $4.50-$17.00 Full bar. Cards: BA, MC, AE, CB. Reservations recommended. Number of rooms 39.

BEAR WALLOW RESORT   *Resort*

For those wishing a relaxed vacation, the features at Bear Wallow are most alluring. Guests may enjoy a hike through the forty acres of redwoods after which a dip in either the swimming pool or the outdoor Jacuzzi whirlpool is thoroughly refreshing. The Alpine Lodge offers a communal lounge with its forty foot fireplace, pool table and bar.

Each of the seven one- and two-bedroom cottages has a fireplace, a fully equipped kitchen, and a private deck surrounded by redwoods and madrones. The cottages, which are named for their locations and views ("Eagle's Nest," "Alpine," "Mountainaire"), are situated among the hills and redwoods so that guests are unaware of their neighbors. If so desired, it is possible to spend time at Bear Wallow entirely secluded.

The restaurant features barbequed steaks and chicken. Bob Hedges tends the small barbeque out by the pool while his wife Roxanne prepares the accompanying Idaho baked potato or rice pilaf and vegetable. All dinners include hot garlic bread, salad, and neopolitan ice cream for dessert. Local Anderson Valley wines make up the wine list; there is no corkage fee.

The 2900 foot Boonville airport is located only four miles away. If you telephone when you land, Bob or Roxanne will be happy to pick you up.

———

Bear Wallow Resort, Manchester Road, Boonville 95415. Telephone (707) 895-3295. Rate: $25.00-$40.00. Restaurant hours: 5:30 p.m.-9 p.m. Wed.-Sun.. Price range: $3.95-$7.95. No cards. Closed January. Reservations recommended. Number of cottages 7. Full bar.

HENDY WOODS STATE PARK   *Campground*

Thanks to the foresight of foundry-owner, Joshua P. Hendy, some ninety years ago, the magnificent coastal redwoods contained in two groves (Big Hendy Grove and Little Hendy Grove) have been preserved from the loggers. After Hendy sold his land to the Masonite Corporation, this firm also saved the virgin woods from the ax and deeded its 405 acres to the state in 1958. The park was opened to the public in 1963 and further acquisitions increased its size to 605 acres.

Most of the area within Hendy Woods is situated on the north slope of Greenwood Ridge, facing Anderson Valley and the towns of Philo and Boonville. Although the virgin groves of *Sequoia sempervirens*, some of which reach over three hundred feet above the forest floor, are the main attractions, madrones, Douglas firs and California laurels are abundant.

The campgrounds at Hendy Woods are located in a wooded area between Big and Little Hendy groves. Each campsite includes a table, a wood stove, a food locker, and a paved parking space. Restrooms and piped drinking water are nearby. There are no showers but they are planned for the future.

The picnic area, located on the south bank of the Navarro River, offers the added attractions of swimming and fishing. Steelhead and salmon fishing can be excellent in the fall and winter. A state sport fishing license is required.

———

Hendy Woods State Park, Star Route 1210, Philo 95466. Telephone (707) 895-3084. Price: $4.00/night. Number of campsites 92. Reservations recommended.

ST. ORRES *Lodging, Dining*

Eight enterprising young men and women from Marin County have recently opened this uniquely attractive lodging and dining facility on the site of the old Seaside Motel just north of Gualala. The two towers rising imposingly out of the tree-studded coastline are reminiscent of Russian-style architecture.

The building and interior were entirely crafted by the owners and local artisans. Especially noteworthy are the heavy oak double doors with colorful stained glass windows that line the wall facing the sea. All the rooms are small, yet tastefully designed and paneled with virgin growth redwood milled in the early 1900's. All eight rooms are on the second floor and share three immaculately clean, tiled bathrooms with skylights.

The cuisine at St. Orres is rapidly gaining a fine reputation up and down the coast. Chef Leif Benson prepares a variety of French entrees ranging from Tournedos Wellington (filet mignon, pate maison, baked in puff pastry with Madiera Sauce) to a seafood salad served in an abalone shell and topped with house dressing. The restaurant itself with three tiers of paned windows is handsomely decorated with hanging plants.

St. Orres, P.O. Box 523, Gualala 95445. Telephone (707) 884-3303. Rates: $35.00-$45.00 including continental breakfast. Restaurant hours: Dinner 6 p.m.-9:30 p.m. Mon.-Fri., 6 p.m.-10 p.m.Sat., 5:30 p.m.-9 p.m. Sun.; Lunch 12 p.m.-2 p.m. Sat. and Sun. only. Price range: Lunch $1.75-$4.50; Dinner $4.50-$10.95. Cards: BA, MC for room only. Number of rooms 8.

HERITAGE HOUSE
Inn

Nestled in along the craggy coastline, the historic Heritage House was built in 1877 by the present owner's grandfather, John Dennen. The old barns are long gone, but the newer buildings blend gracefully with both the architecture of the farmhouse and the surrounding landscape.

Most of the accommodations are in the individual cottages scattered throughout the hillside. Each room is decorated differently to reflect the name inspired by early buildings of the area, such as ''Schoolhouse,'' ''Stable,'' ''Country Store,'' and ''Ice Cream Parlor.'' The furnishings include many valued antiques from the immediate vicinity. The Dennens have tried not only to preserve some history and hospitality of an era but also to provide refuge and privacy amid luxurious surroundings.

The room rates are based on a ''modified American plan'' which includes breakfast and dinner. The lavish breakfasts offer a buffet of fruits, juices and cereals as well as a full American breakfast of bacon and eggs served at the table. Dinners vary nightly and are on a first come, first seated basis. Jackets and ties are preferred dinner attire. The wine list is one of the most extensive in the area.

Heritage House, Little River 95456. Telephone (707) 937-5885. Rates: Single $38.00-$68.00, Double $50.00-$90.00. Closed Dec. and Jan.. Restaurant hours: Breakfast 8 a.m.-10 a.m.; Dinner 6 p.m.-8 p.m.. Price range: Breakfast $3.50-$4.50; Dinner $8.00-$9.00. No cards. No pets. Reservations required. 50 Units.

LITTLE RIVER INN   *Inn*

The Little River Inn accommodations comprise rooms in the main house, the new Hilltop Annex, and some cottage units. The attic rooms of the house are the least expensive, yet the privacy given by the casual cottages, when available, is well worth the higher rate.

The 1853 white frame house standing prominently at the edge of Highway 1 is the original home of lumber and shipping overseer Silas Coombs. Today the Maine-style mansion houses offices, lobby, restaurant, and the few attic rooms, all luxuriously decorated with antiques. For those wishing to experience the sensation of early California, these rooms are recommended.

The cottage units and the contemporary Hilltop Annex which provide the other two types of accommodations are outfitted in eclectic collections of more modern furniture. Every room offers a panoramic view of the sea.

The Inn operates on the European plan. However, the rustic bar and dining rooms where the chef specializes in steaks and seafood are open to the public. A nine-hole golf course attended by a PGA professional and sheltered by eucalyptus trees is available to both guests and passers-by.

———

Little River Inn, Highway 1, Little River 95456. Telephone (707) 937-5942. Room rates for two: $24.00-$60.00 year round. Restaurant hours: 7:30 a.m.-2 p.m.; 6 p.m.-10 p.m.. Price range: $2.00-$10.50. No cards. Reservations advised. Total number of units 45.

VAN DAMME STATE PARK   *Campground, Hiking*

John and Louise Van Damme, a Flemish couple from Belgium, settled at Little River in the 1860's. Their son, Charles, who operated the San Rafael-Richmond Ferry, fondly remembered the old mill town of Little River. His concern that the beach, a favorite picnic spot, remain available for public use, prompted him to purchase forty acres to be used by the people on the coast. At his death in 1930 the land was deeded to the state. Additional acreage was purchased to create Van Damme State Park, now 1826 acres.

The park, in addition to being a good look at the natural world of the coast, reaches back into the canyon, following the long narrow river into the mystical regions of Sword Fern Canyon and the Pygmy Forest. Here thickets of gnarled and lichen-encrusted Mendocino cypress trees, some as old as sixty years, grow just a few feet tall and less than half an inch in diameter. Dwarf Bolander pines range to fifteen feet. The fern growth spreads up from the river on both sides for approximately three miles.

There are now 82 campsites within the park, and some of these are shaded. Restrooms with flush toilets and hot-water showers are nearby. Summer nature programs covering plants and wildlife of the area are a popular feature. There are bicycle trails as well as hiking trails.

———

Van Damme State Park, Highway 1, Little River 95456. Telephone (707) 937-5855. Price: $4.00/night. Reservations recommended. Number of campsites 82.

MACCALLUM HOUSE   *Inn, Restaurant*

This splendid three story Victorian was constructed in 1882 by lumber magnate William H. Kelly as a gift for his newlywed daughter Daisy MacCallum.

San Franciscans, William and Sue Norris, purchased the property from the MacCallum family in 1974 complete with all the original furnishings and began transforming it into a charming inn. The Norisses wallpapered the bedrooms with Victorian era prints and covered the antique beds with matching homemade quilts. Even the old greenhouse, gazebo, and water tower have become comfortable guest houses. Bathrooms, as per the boarding house tradition, are communal.

Dining at the MacCallum House is truly a delightful experience. Guests relax around two stone fireplaces while enjoying dishes prepared by chef Robert Parks. The house specialty, rack of lamb, is baked in mustards and herbs and served with Dijon and sherry sauce. When in season the poached salmon filets with Bernaise, almonds and capers is a must. Generous entrees are flawlessly presented with freshly baked bread and sweet butter, tossed salad, two vegetables and potatoes au gratin or rice and mushrooms. A limited wine list prompts eonophiles to bring their own bottles.

———

MacCallum House, 740 Albion St., Mendocino 95460. Telephone (707) 937-0289. Rates: $27.50-$34.50 double with continental breakfast. Reservations suggested. Rooms: 15. Restaurant (707) 937-5763. Hours: 7-10 p.m. Tues.-Sun. Dinner $3.95-$9.95. Full bar service. Cards: AE, BA, MC. Dining room open Apr.-Dec..

SEA ROCK MOTEL   *Motel*

The Sea Rock Motel, set into an oceanside hill, is a self-service establishment. Some of the rooms have kitchens and some have fireplaces, but there are no telephones and no televisions. The cottages, which house several rooms under one roof, face the sea. Along with a key to your room you receive a key to Sea Rock's private access to Agate Beach. The Sea Rock offers by far the most reasonable rates for such privacy in the Mendocino area.

———

Sea Rock Motel, 11101 No. Lansing St., Mendocino 95460. Telephone (707) 937-5517. Rates: $16.50-$33.00 for two people. Cards: BA, MC. Reservations advised. Number of units 11.

MENDOCINO HOTEL   *Hotel, Restaurant*

The bright yellow Mendocino Hotel stands out among Main Street's row of historical structures facing the traveler driving north on Highway 1 towards Mendocino. The hotel has been completely rebuilt since its founding in 1878 and redecorated in true Victorian style. The lobby itself is impressive with its authentic antiques and luxuriously colored carpets and chairs. The adjoining bar is similarly decorated to accent the old church window in the ceiling. What a relaxing setting in which to enjoy an Irish coffee while sitting in a comfortable chair and gazing out to sea!

The rooms upstairs are small but elegantly and individually decorated in 19th century style. Some beds have canopies, and some have heavy carved oak headboards. Although every room has a small washstand, most guests are required to share bathrooms.

Now that the Larsens of The Restaurant in Fort Bragg have taken over organization of the kitchen, great dishes should be emerging from it. Both menus offer seafood, meats and poultry, and the wine list is a selection of two dozen North Coast wines.

Mendocino Hotel, 45080 Main St., Mendocino 95460. Telephone (707) 937-0511. Room rates: $25.00-$55.00, all double occupancy. Includes breakfast. Restaurant hours: Lunch 11:30 a.m.-2:30 p.m.; Sunday brunch 10:30 a.m.-2:30 p.m.; Dinner 5:30 p.m.-9:30 p.m. daily. Price range: Lunch $1.65-$4.50; Dinner $5.25-$8.75. Cards: BA, MC. Reservations advised. Number of rooms 23.

HARBOR LITE LODGE   *Motel*

The rustic redwood exterior of the Harbor Lite Lodge fits well with the rugged Mendocino coastline just south of Fort Bragg.

Hosts Freda and Wayne Moilanen offer spacious rooms with queen-size beds and color television. Most have private balconies overlooking the harbor. For the adventuresome, hillside trails lead down to the village or along the rocks to the beach. By way of contrast, guests are invited to enjoy the Scandinavian sauna or the sheltered deck provided for lounging.

Harbor Lite Lodge, 120 No. Harbor Drive, Fort Bragg 95437. Telephone (707) 964-0221. Rates: Single $20.00 Double $23.00-$28.00. Cards: BA, MC, AE, DC. Number of units 70.

MENDOCINO COUNTY

NORTHERN SONOMA COUNTY

SOUTHERN SONOMA COUNTY

The

Wineries

MILL CREEK VINEYARDS

CAMBIASO WINERY

SOTOYOME WINERY

FOPPIANO VINEYARDS

SONOMA VINEYARDS

LANDMARK VINEYARDS

HOP KILN WINERY

DAVIS BYNUM WINERY

KORBEL & BROS.

MARK WEST VINEYARDS

SWAN VINEYARDS

RUSSIAN RIVER VINEYARDS

MARTINI & PRATI WINES

SCALE 1:125 000

5000   5000   10000 15000 20000 25000 30000 35000 40000 45000 FEET

CONTOUR INTERVAL 200 FEET
DOTTED LINES REPRESENT 40-FOOT CONTOURS
DATUM IS MEAN SEA LEVEL

TRUE NORTH
MAGNETIC NORTH
17½°

SANTA ROSA

CHATEAU ST. JEAN

KENWOOD VINEYARDS

GRAND CRU VINEYARDS

VALLEY OF THE MOON WINERY

HANZELL VINEYARDS

HACIENDA CELL

BUENA VISTA WINERY

SEBASTIANI

GUNDLACH BUNDSCHU WINE CO

Z-D WINERY

Southern
Sonoma
Wineries

Gundlach Bundschu Wine Co.

In the foothills of the Huichica Mountains to the east of the town of Sonoma is the Gundlach Bundschu Wine Co. Nestled in the historic Sonoma Valley, it has been recognized as one of California's most venerable names in wine. In 1858, the winery rose to prominence due largely to the intelligence and imagination of its founders Germans Jacob Gundlach and Emil Dresel.

Originally the pair had founded the distinguished wine firm of J. Gundlach & Co. The company made wine from grapes grown in the vineyards located at the winery estate in Sonoma known as the Rhine Farm. In 1864, Gundlach and Dresel were joined by two other enterprising Californians, Charles Bundschu and Harry Winkle. Together the four men created the Gundlach Bundschu Wine Co.

The original 400-acre plot planted at the Rhine Farm was made up of varietals such as Riesling, Traminer, Gutedel, Kleinberger, Zinfandel, Semillion, Petite Sirah, Cabernet Sauvignon and Merlot. The wines were sold commercially under the Bachus wine label.

In the late 1850's when the stone winery was built, it was designed to handle 150,000 gallons, a magnificent volume in those days. For nearly 50 years, business continued to expand and the foursome developed successful wholesale and retail outlets in both New York and San Francisco. In San Francisco, the Gundlach Bundschu Wine Co. had a three-story wine vault on Bryant Street housing old and rare vintages. During the 1906 earthquake, these then-famous wine cellars were completely destroyed. The only significant traces that were left after the fire were charred barrel hoops which lay in the rubble of the crumbled foundations.

In the aftermath of the earthquake, the owners of Gundlach Bundschu Wine Co. attempted to rebuild their wine fortune. Due to the experimental work in 1875 of Julius Dresel, one of the founders, the vineyards at the Rhine Farm were not affected by pylloxera, a vine pest which destroys the roots of the grapevine. Dresel was successful in grafting disease-prone vines onto pylloxera resistant rootstocks. The vineyards were healthy and productive. In 1918 with the coming of Prohibition, the winery was closed down, but the vineyards were kept in production.

Over the next 40 or so years the vineyards were maintained. Wine grapes were sold commercially to Louis Martini and Almaden. The winery, which was abandoned, eventually burned down.

In 1964, the great-great-grand children of founder Charles Bundschu, then and now living in the rustic stone mansion (designed by William Farr who is also the architect of Jack London's Wolf House), began making wine for fun. One Halloween night, Jim Bundschu, Jacob's great-great-grandson, and John Merritt, a friend, made a promise to each other to revive the Gundlach Bundschu Wine Co. name and make wine under the original Baccus wine label.

By 1968, the old vineyards were replanted. Grafts from some of the original varieties were used.

Z-D Winery

Z-D Winery is named for its founders Gino Zepponi and Norman de Leuze. The brown, wooden barn which serves as the winery building is located on the outskirts of Sonoma on Burndale Rd.

Zepponi and de Leuze first met in the sixties while employed in the field of engineering. Both gentlemen were then dabbling in home winemaking. In time, they discovered their common interest which had been handed down to them from their respective families. Since his youth, Zepponi had made wine under the tutelage of his father, a winemaker from Italy. De Leuze acquired his knowledge from his grandfather, also an engineer, who had managed distilleries in Mexico and California.

In the autumn of 1969, the two partners, who share all work equally from "winemaking to floor sweeping" crushed six tons of grapes. This was equivalent to 900 gallons. Starting out on a meagre budget, they improvised with an old wooden crusher and hand-operated basket press supplied by the Zepponi family. Since that first golden, fall day, they have increased their production to around 1,000 cases a year.

"Our aim is to produce two great wines: Pinot Chardonnay and Pinot Noir. We want to continue as a small family-operated, premium winery, always paying attention to detail," summarizes de Leuze.

Because Z-D Winery is so very small, the partners place great importance on the quality of grapes and the district from which they come. The winery owners purchase grapes from three vineyards owned by Rene di Rosa: Winery Lake, St. Clair and Zepponi: La Casa Zepponi Vineyards. The vines of di Rosa and St. Clair are located in the Carneros district at the southern junction of Sonoma and Napa counties. Zepponi's vineyard is located near the winery just 1 mile south of Sonoma. The weather in the Carneros area is characterized by cool breezes and bay fogs which stimulate early ripening of the berries. Production from the vines grown in this area average two tons to the acre which is a small, quality yield. Pinot Noir from this region tends to be very dark red in color and full on the palate. Chardonnay tastes rich and fruity.

All the Z-D wines come across as extremely dry. Made of 100 per cent varietals, they are all vintage-dated and vineyard-identified. In addition to the Pinot Noir and Chardonnay, the winery produces a very dry and spicy Gewurztraminer and a raspberryish Zinfandel. The wines are available in small quantities at the winery and in Bay Area retail shops.

Once the grapes are selected during the harvest, they are weighed and crushed immediately, leaving stems on the berries. The grapes are fermented in small batches for quality control purposes. The wines are then aged in small 50 and 60 gallon barrels comprised of American white oak and French Limousin and Nevers oak.

"Z-D Winery ages its wines in the same barrels in which they are made. We virtually do nothing to the wine, hence, they are totally natural wines which our customers must realize require proper storage for aging," comments partner Zepponi, who is also a winery systems engineering and enology consultant.

Sebastiani Vineyards

Sebastiani vineyards lie on the historic locus of the first vineyard cultivated north of San Francisco. The vines were planted in 1825 by Franciscan padres at the Mission San Francisco de Solano, in Sonoma. Following the Act of Secularization, which ended the Church's reign over the mission system and replaced it with Mexican authority, the vineyard was acquired by General Mariano G. Vallejo.

Samuele Sebastiani had been born into a peasant family who toiled in the vineyards of Tuscany. Short of formal education (he never did learn to write English) and impatient with a sharecropper's existence, in 1892 he borrowed money for steerage to California. He worked in the vegetable gardens of San Francisco, then moved north to Sonoma. A diligent worker, fond of physical exertion, he bought a stout cart and a team of horses and began hauling cobblestones from the quarries in the Mayacamas Mountains east of town. Sonoma's City Hall, a regional landmark, was built by Italian immigrants, who Sebastiani sponsored, and largely with cobblestones Sebastiani quarried and hauled.

In 1904 he purchased an old horse barn-turned-winery at the northeast corner of town and the Franciscan/Vallejo vineyard across the street. Visitors to the winery today are shown the hand crusher, hand basket press, and 501-gallon redwood tank Samuele and his uncle used to make the winery's first Zinfandel. When the wine was aged, Samuele sold it door-to-door from barrels on his horse-drawn wagon.

During the unwelcome intrusion of Prohibition he kept the winery alive by producing sacramental and medicinal wines. He also set up a fruit and vegetable cannery next door to keep his employees at work and protect his investment. At Repeal Samuele's youngest son, August, left college to help run the family business. He learned to make the big, sharp on the tongue, full-bodied reds that typify Italian wines. And, as was the custom then, the wines were sold to larger wine merchants like Lachman & Jacobi, who resold them under a myriad of different labels, none of which directly mentioned the wines' true origins.

After Samuele's death in 1944 the complexion of the winery changed, slowly at first. By the early fifties August had begun to produce wines for his own label. The story leading up to the move is best told by August himself:

"One day my wife, Sylvia, returned from an afternoon of bridge. She commented on the pale dry cocktail sherry her hostess had served and asked why we did not make such a wine. It was my wine, under someone else's label! It really bothered me that I couldn't even get credit from my own wife. That's when I knew it was time for a change."

August is proud that both his sons have joined him in running the winery. Sam's primary obligations are management, but he likes to get into the vineyards as often as his hectic schedule will allow. Don, the young-

Aging Cellars at Sebastiani Vineyards

est of August's three children, is learning the business by working as his father's assistant. Their brother-in-law, Dick Cuneo, is the winery's controller.

August has gained a sort of notoriety for the custom-tailored, blue and white striped, bib overalls he habitually wears. But it's no pose. The man is a farmer by love and a businessman by necessity.

Anyone taken in by August's comfortable dress is liable to be taken for a fascinating--August is charming and witty--but financially unrewarding ride. For August Sebastiani couples a vast reservoir of knowledge and experience with a keen, native sense of timing. Before the rise of consumer sophistication in the early seventies, he had already begun vintage dating his top varietals. When the demand came, he had the wines. When prices got out of hand, he hit the market like a tidal wave with varietals in half gallons at markedly lower prices. In 1972 he started an American tradition, albeit borrowed from France, with his Nouveau Gamay Beaujolais, a fruity, tantalizing red meant to be drunk within months of its production. People make special trips to Sonoma to obtain the Nouveau when it is released annually on November 15th.

From a position of producing less than 300,000 cases of wine a year in the early seventies, Sebastiani Vineyards now produces well over a million cases each vintage. And as long as the Sebastiani name has been known to wine lovers, the name Barbera has been an appendage to it. It is the wine that links the American Sebastianis with their European homeland.

The Sebastiani Barberas, like many Italian wines (though *not*, curiously, those made with Barbera), are designed to stand up to the most heavily spiced of foods. The label says "Bold and Robust," and so the wines are.

The Sebastianis offer a complete line of table, dessert, aperitif, and sparkling wines. To name them all would be superfluous, but a few deserve special mention. One is their Solera Cream Sherry, dubbed "Amore." The Sebastianis maintain an outdoor solera of 2400 50-gallon oak barrels to fractionally blend and age their sherries. The sun's heat bakes the wines slowly, caramelizing existing sugars, giving the Cream Sherry a deep, creamy, amber color, a thicker consistency, and delightful, nut-like flavors. In 1977 the winery released another fractionally blended wine that had almost been forgotten, it had been in the winery so long. Labeled Angelica Antigua, a mere 363 cases were bottled, individually numbered, and sold at $30 a crack. The wine reminds one of peach cobbler. Another showcase wine is Pinot Noir Blanc, subtitled "Eye of the Swan" for its copper cast, like unto the eye color of a Black Australian Swan in August's aviary (he is an internationally known breeder of rare doves).

As the winery grows inevitably larger, the Sebastianis continue to expand their wood and bottle aging facilities. While many whites and light-bodied reds are sold soon after bottling, the heavier reds continue to receive two or three years in redwood and oak and an additional year in the bottle before release.

Buena Vista Winery

In a naturally wooded glen beside the Arroyo Seco Creek east of Sonoma stands an imposing grey stone structure. Over the entrance is a smart red and gold coat of arms with a drawn sword above a king's crown. Below are two large redwood doors bolted closed with iron latches. The historic doors open to reveal the legend of Buena Vista and the House of Haraszthy.

Buena Vista is the oldest winery in the Sonoma Valley. Founded in 1857 by the celebrated Col. Agoston Haraszthy de Moskea, it has been highly acclaimed as the home of California winemaking.

All his life, Haraszthy had a passionate involvement in the cause of liberty and justice, and it was his concern for conditions of the common Hungarian under an oppressive monarchy that caused his exile. Though a high-ranking army officer, Haraszthy found it necessary to escape from his native land in 1840 and flee to the United States.

Soon after landing on the Eastern seaboard, the ever restless Haraszthy headed westward. Along the way he experimented with vineyards in Sauk, Wisconsin and later on in San Diego, California. His engaging personality impressed people everywhere. He left his name on buildings, towns, parks, schools, roads, bridges and churches. However, it wasn't until he settled in Sonoma that he reached his true potential as a grower of quality grapes and a producer of fine wines.

While Haraszthy was living near San Francisco, General Mariano Vallejo invited the colonel to visit his country estate, Lachryma Monte (Tear of the Mountain) and taste the wines of the district. Impressed with the overall quality of the wines, the colonel began purchasing hillside acreage beneath the Mayacamas Mountains, where he planted vineyards and constructed a magnificent Pompeian villa. Today the site of his house, which looked westward to San Pablo Bay, is included in the vineyards belonging to Hacienda Wine Cellars.

From the beginning, Buena Vista Winery built an outstanding reputation based on its willingness to experiment with imported varietals, its use of then sophisticated equipment and its application of advanced technologies. The operation was unique in every way. It was well-equipped with automated crusher-stemmers, redwood holding tanks, quality fermenters and small oak cooperage. Two hand-hewn caves were built into the limestone hillside. During that time, Haraszthy popularized the Zinfandel and Muscat grape, successfully challenging the current assumption that the Mission grape was all that could produce wine in California.

In June 1861, Haraszthy left on a trip for Europe, which eventually would have profound effects on the California wine industry. He returned with 200,000 plants of nearly 500 varieties from the major wine districts. Later on these vines became the basis of the California wine industry.

Buena Vista began as Haraszthy's private, family-

Old Champagne Cellars at Buena Vista

owned enterprise. It later incorporated and became the Buena Vista Horticultural Society and offered stock to the public. By the 1860's after continual internal strife and lack of payments, Haraszthy resigned as head of the company and left California for Nicaragua. Receiving a commission from the government of that country to manufacture rum, he planted sugar cane and built a distillery. Quite unexpectedly, he died, reportedly drowning. He left a son Gaza to manage the estate in South America, and he left sons Attila and Arpad to run the winery in North America.

In the years that followed, the winery excelled in its production of quality dry table wines and champagne. By the late 1890's the majority of the vineyards (and those throughout the county) were destroyed by pylloxera, a plague caused by a pesty bug which eats away at the root of the vines. No sooner was the land re-planted than it was hit by the 1906 earthquake. The heavy tremors collapsed the hillside tunnels and destroyed the winery's inventory of wine. From that time on, the winery remained closed for almost four decades.

In 1940, Frank Bartholomew, then a rising young executive and now chairman of the board emeritus of United Press International, acquired the abandoned winery and vineyards. With confidence, he restored Buena Vista to its original grandeur, renovating the winery and landscaping the grounds. Aided by the noted enologist Andre Tchelistcheff, Bartholomew was able to rebuild the winery's commercial name. Through his many contacts throughout the United States and Europe, Batholomew saw that the Buena Vista label was included on the wine lists of the better restaurants, hotels and inns around the world. The public responded favorably to the Zinfandel, Green Hungarian and Gewurztraminer. By the late forties, the winery was registered as an official historical site.

In 1968, Young's Market Co., a Los Angeles wholesale wine and liquor firm, assumed ownership of Bartholomew's interest which included the original buildings and 15 acres of Gewurztraminer and Riesling grapes. Realizing the historical significance of the purchase, President Philip C. Gaspar hired two descedants of Haraszthy to work at the winery: his grandson Jan and his great grandson Vallejo. This gesture has provided the link between the original Buena Vista and the Haraszthys of today. The new facility is realized in the transition of the winery from 20,000 cases a year to a projected 200,000 cases a year.

Change is evident not only in the size of the winery but its new location. The new Buena Vista complex lies just across the Sonoma County line in Napa County on Ramal Rd. Nearby there are 750 acres of vineyard, an excellent source of red wine grapes. The climate here is particularly suited to early ripening varieties.

"With our new facilities, we want to produce the best wine from the best grapes we can grow," says Chilean-born technical director and winemaster Rene Lacasia.

Today the wines of Buena Vista are characterized by a combination of the old and the new. Winemaking goes on at both winery sites. Buena Vista Winery will continue to make its extensive line of table wines, dessert wines, sparkling wines and special bottlings.

Hacienda Wine Cellars

Two stone pillars mark the approach to Hacienda Wine Cellars, situated in the western foothills of the Mayacamas Mountains. The road to Hacienda curves by the site of Agoston Haraszthy's Italian villa through the vineyards to an avenue of pines outside the winery.

In 1940, Frank Bartholomew, then an executive and now chairman of the board emeritus of United Press International, bought the old Buena Vista estate. With the help of noted winemaker Andre' Tchelistcheff, he re-established the name in the commercial marketplace. Rapid growth eventually brought Bartholomew to sell the Buena Vista Winery and 18 acres of vineyards to a group from Los Angeles. He kept 450 acres, some of which he is developing for his own purposes as Hacienda Wine Cellars.

He created a new tan-colored winery with tile roof and outdoor balconies in the early Spanish architectural style. In the past, the building had many identities—as an industrial farm, as a proposed wine museum and as a rest home. In the early seventies, it was reconstructed with redwood timbers once used in Ft. Baker on San Francisco Bay. The downstairs was designed with 100 private bins, kept under lock and key by owners who house their wines at the winery.

Bartholomew explains Hacienda Wine Cellars as an experiment ''in quality and nothing else.'' Because the winery is very small, producing just 4,000 cases a year, extra time can be taken in the vineyard and in the winery to produce wines which are stylistically compatible to the tastes of the modern consumer.

Bartholomew expresses his thoughts, ''I understand the American palate. I share the interest of professionals in laboratory analysis. I understand what Americans like and dislike. We have technical breakdowns, but we add the pleasure quotient. Did you like that? A wine can be technically perfect and still not give pleasure.''

So far Hacienda has 60 acres of vineyard developed. The plots are located in select, sunny patches throughout the estate. Continuing research has identified those varieties which do best in a particular location.

Hacienda Wine Cellars puts great pride in making and storing its white wines entirely in stainless steel. The Chardonnay Clair de Lune is an example of a wine created in a lighter, fruitier style with no flavors imparted by wood.

The reds are handled more traditionally, fermented in redwood and aged in 60-gallon French Never oak casks. Each wine is aged according to the conditions of the harvest and the marketplace. The reds are produced with extra color and tannin to develop flavor complexities.

Emphasizing Hacienda's single-minded devotion to palate-pleasing wine production, winemaker Steve MacRostie exclaims, ''Basically we are following our own rules. We believe in good, sound, clean winemaking.''

Hanzell Vineyards

The road winds and turns around an oak, olive and oleander, through trellised vineyards to a promontory overlooking the Sonoma Valley. There one finds Hanzell Vineyards, engulfed much of the year in brilliant pink bougainvillea.

In the late forties, James D. Zellerbach, heir to the San Francisco paper fortune and one-time ambassador to Italy, set out to find the perfect site for a vineyard and winery. An admitted Francophile, he dazzled Californians with his plan for creating unsurpassable Burgundian style wines. After much searching, he selected a 200-acre parcel with an old stone farmhouse and apple orchards near Sonoma.

In 1952, the land was cleared and terraced for five acres of Chardonnay and nine acres of Pinot Noir. The gently sloping vineyards were planted on redhill clay loam with a southwestern exposure. In 1957 San Francisco architects Porter and Steinwedell drew detailed plans for the winery with architectural features simulating Clos de Vougeot in Burgundy. Dubbed Hanzell, the name was a combination of (Mrs.) Hannah Zellerbach's first name and James Zellerbach's last name.

Nearly two decades later, following Zellerbach's death, his wine estate fell into the hands of Mr. and Mrs. Douglas Shaw of Sacramento. They maintained the winery until 1975. In March of that year, young Australian heiress Barabara de Brye, a resident of England and sometimes the United States, became associated with the winery. She plans to plant 12 more acres of vineyard, which will increase yearly production to 3,500 cases.

Since its conception, Hanzell has been an innovator of the unusual. Back in the fifties, it was one of the first wineries to introduce the chateau concept of growing and making only two wines, Chardonnay and Pinot Noir.

Hanzell is unique because the vineyards and winery are designed on a small scale to insure quality. At harvest, a professional crew comes in and hand selects the 17 acres of grapes. The grapes are fermented in one-ton-lots in 298 gallon, custom-made stainless steel fermenters.

The Chardonnay is crushed and allowed to sit on the skins for a short time before pressing. It ferments for eight to nine weeks at 55 degrees Farenheit, then is racked and allowed to settle. The Chardonnay ages for six to 12 months in 60-gallon Limousin oak barrels and one year in bottle.

The Pinot Noir is crushed, destemmed, fermented for five days to no color then pressed. The free run and light press are combined, then racked and settled. The Pinot Noir spends two and a half years in wood and one to one and a half years in bottle.

In the early days, Brad Webb was the winemaker. Since 1973, Robert Sessions has been the do-everything winemaster, vineyard manager and winery manager,

"Everything is done with care and quality," remarks Sessions. "The Hanzell philosophy follows a Burgundian tradition of winemaking with liberal use of technology."

Valley of the Moon Winery

Situated on Madrone Road, in the Valley of the Moon beside the Sonoma Creek, these historic vineyards have witnessed a colorful past.

Originally a portion of the Agua Caliente Rancho granted by the Mexican government to Lazaro Pena, the land was purchased by General M.G. Vallejo and later 640 acres were given to his children's music teacher in exchange for their piano lessons. In 1851, Joseph Hooker took over this portion of the Ranch and planted a vineyard using Indian and Chinese labor. He was also appointed road-overseer for Sonoma County and ran for the State Assembly. However, at the outbreak of the Civil War, he sold his property and left Sonoma for the East. There he gained fame as ''Fighting Joe Hooker'' of the Union Army.

Eli T. Sheppard, former American consul to Tientsin, China, and later an advisor in International Law to the Japanese Emperor, bought the property in 1883 and named it Madrone Vineyards. He added French vines to the vineyard and was written up in several books of that time as one of the growers whose names are almost as well known as the wines of Sonoma themselves. He is also recorded as one the the winemakers of the Sonoma Valley. Because of poor health, he sold the vineyard to United States Senator George Hearst and retired to San Francisco in 1888.

Senator Hearst became well known for the fine wines that were produced from his Sonoma vineyard. He added Medoc and Gironda grapes to the vineyard and used two stone wine cellars that together could hold 244,000 gallons of wine. His vineyard was described as one of the finest in the State, and he proudly served his own wines and brandy to his guests in Washington, D.C.. Unfortunately, after Senator Hearst's death, the vineyards and winery were sold and they changed hands many times until 1922.

In 1922, Louis Engelberg purchased the Madrone Vineyards. He operated the vineyards through the prohibition and depression years, although the winery was not in operation. Engelberg sold the grapes from the vineyards to other wineries and maintained the high quality expected from Madrone Vineyards.

When Enrico Parducci and Peitro Domenici purchased Madrone Vineyards in 1941, the winery had fallen into disuse. However, they were able to start production in 1942. Since then, Valley of the Moon Winery has been well known for their bulk wines: Semillon, Chablis, Vin Rose', Claret, Burgundy, and Zinfandel. In 1974, under the management of Harry Parducci, Enrico's son, Valley of the Moon Winery introduced their 100% Sonoma Valley varietals. These wines, which are entirely made of the grape variety named on the label include: French Colombard, Semillon, Zinfandel, and Pinot Noir. These wines are made with grapes from their own vineyards under the supervision of Otto Toschi, winemaker at Valley of the Moon Winery for over thirty years.

Grand Cru Vineyards

At the end of Vintage Lane in the town of Glen Ellen one can find Grand Cru Vineyards. It is located in the shadow of the Mayacamas Mountains on a parallel with Oakville in Napa County.

Grand Cru Vineyards was established in 1970. Its name originates from the French appellation controllee designation meaning literally "great vineyard," but in fact designating the finest vintages. The A-frame winery sits on top of the stone foundations of the now rehabilitated Lamoines cellars.

During the international settlement of Sonoma County, Francois Lamoines and his family settled in the Sonoma Valley. They erected a stately mansion and winery with a vineyard containing imported varietals. By the 1900's the winery was bought by the Mancuso family. From their Zinfandel acreage, they sold wines in bulk and under private label. Although theoretically the winery was closed during Prohibition, it is rumored that wine activities did take place. After that era, the winery was reopened and stayed in business with little notoriety until closed in the forties. For the next 20 years there was no activity at the winery and it was closed until it was purchased by Grand Cru people.

In the late sixties Robert Magnani and Allen Ferrera, two engineering associates, decided to go into the wine business. Enthusiastically, they formed a corporation and they took on the responsibilities as winemaker and manager respectively.

As a youngster Magnani had learned winemaking from his uncle who had worked with Charles Forni, the winemaker and owner of what is now Freemark Abbey Winery. Ferrera gained practical layman's experience as a summer helper at Mayacamas Vineyards.

All the work at Grand Cru Vineyards has been shared by owners and friends of the winery. Seven vaulted concrete rooms, once used as storage tanks, were cut open for floor space. Once expansion is completed, the facility will feature a tasting room with verandas and walkways above an enclosed fermentation site. Adjacent to the area will be cellars for aging champagne and wine.

Besides the 25 acres of 80-year-old Zinfandel vines in Glen Ellen, owned by Grand Cru, the winery obtains grapes from the Garden Creek Ranch on the west side of Alexander Valley. The Gewurztraminer and Pinot Noir are grown on the valley floor while the Cabernet Sauvignon comes from the terraced hillsides.

The winery's selection includes Cabernet Sauvignon, Zinfandel, Gewurztraminer, a dessert Gewurztraminer and sparkling wine produced from Pinot Noir. All the wines are fermented in custom-made, temperature-controlled stainless steel tanks and aged in oak casks and barrels.

"I am basically obsessed with trying to get as much varietal character into the wine as possible. The wine should taste and smell intensely aromatic," stresses Magnani, winemaker.

Chateau St. Jean

Chateau St. Jean rests at the foot of Adobe Canyon in Kenwood, California, with Mt. Hood to the east and the Sugarloaf Ridge to the west. As one of the most spectacular new winery complexes in the Sonoma Valley, this 200-acre vineyard estate is the former residence of Maude Goff, a member of a wealthy Minneapolis mining family.

The white Mediterranean-style chateau contains the offices and tasting room. Designed around a courtyard and pool, the house looks out on new vineyards and formal gardens. Outside the drawing room are an arbor covered with vines and several ponds in the shape of the Great Lakes. The grounds flourish with palm, pine, pomegrante, fig, coffee and tea. Of special interest is an unusual apple tree given to the Goffs by Luther Burbank.

Several years ago, brothers Robert and Edward Merzoian, who both have vineyards in Visalia and Porterville respectively, resolved to go into the premium winemaking business. Joined by W. Kenneth Sheffield they purchased the Kenwood, California, property. In 1974, Richard L. Arrowood joined them as winemaker.

The new winery complex is designed to follow the French style of architecture found in the main house. The building includes a barrel room, a fermentation chamber and a champagne cellar.

The mountain and valley vineyards cover 80 acres. During a typical growing season, the upland weather is free of fog while the lowlands receive a great deal of fog. From acre to acre, the soil varies from sandy loam to pure rock, well suited for quality grapes.

Chateau St. Jean will produce small lots from historic vineyards such as Wildwood Vineyards in the Sonoma Valley which is owned by Arthur Kunde. In 1975, the winery crushed 12 acres of what is said to be some of the oldest Cabernet Sauvignon grapes in California, formerly sold to Beaulieu Vineyards. Arrowood has arranged to preserve five of the original acres; the rest of the vineyards were destroyed.

Chateau St. Jean has released several commendable wines indicative of its "goal to achieve quality." The line of white wines include a Pinot Blanc, Sauvignon Blanc, Johannisberg Riesling, several vineyard-designated Chardonnays and Champagne.

The whites are uniformly cold-fermented with some skin contact to produce added color. Afterwards they are dejuiced and centrifuged before racked and aged for a clearer, fruitier effect. Most of the whites see time in small oak cooperage with the exception of those with residual sugar, a natural sweetness in the wine.

"With the white wines I want to produce wines with plenty of intense fruit," comments Arrowood, winemaker. "With the Chardonnay I want to make a clean, fresh wine with a distinct Chardonnay aroma which will last seven to ten years."

The red wines are fermented at a warmer temperature for about a week and a half to allow the juice to dry on the skins for added tannin. All the reds are aged in small 60-gallon French and 50-gallon American oak.

Kenwood Vineyards

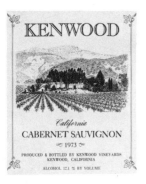

The rustic gabled barn and wood-frame California bungalow are reminders of the pioneer history of Kenwood Vineyards. Set against the foothills of Sugarloaf Ridge, the winery and ranch look across vineyards and orchards to the Sonoma Valley.

After the turn-of-the century, Julius Pagani, a native of Italy who had generations of winemakers in his family tree, settled in Kenwood. He made red and white wine, which he sold in bulk to Napa and Sonoma wineries and in gallon jugs under the Pagani label to friends, neighbors and travelers.

In 1970 after Pagani's death and after his heirs opted out of the wine business the property came to the attention of a group of Bay Area wine enthusiasts, mostly involved in other professions. Martin Lee, his sons Marty and Mike Lee; John Sheela, Bob Kozlowski and Neil Knott. They bought the land, buildings and winemaking equipment. Kozlowski, a wine hobbyist and chemist became winemaker, assisted by Mike Lee.

Change took place slowly. The mixed burgundy vineyard (composed of many varieties) was uprooted and replanted with Johannisberg Riesling. A decision was made to lease as many other vineyards as needed within the Sonoma Valley area.

As is often true on European farms, the physical appearance does not always reflect the quality of the wine. Such is the case at Kenwood Vineyards. Outwardly, the buildings appear rustic and almost run-down.

Inside is an attractive redwood tasting room with stained glass windows and a ceiling which is made from grape stakes. At the back of the property is a large wood and galvanized building which houses the stainless steel jacketed fermenters, the redwood fermenters, the upright and small oak cooperage.

Kenwood Vineyards employs the "cuvee" (which means cask, vat or lot in French) method of winemaking. Small batches of a particular variety of wine are fermented individually then put in cask. As the wines mature, they are carefully analyzed to be sure that they develop the desired fruits and flavors. The winery tries to make the wines as naturally as possible. Most of the white wines are held in stainless steel with the exception of the Chardonnay which ages in Yugoslavian oak. The reds are aged in small, 60-gallon American white oak barrels.

"Our present course of action is to reach between 20,000 and 25,000 cases a year," explains Marty Lee, national sales manager. "We want to remain flexible in our policies. We want to be able to select and choose different Sonoma vineyards at will. As any winery, we would like to be known as the best for producing quality red wines in Sonoma County.

The winery is now streamlining its line of wines to feature Chardonnay, Chenin Blanc, Cabernet Sauvignon, Pinot Noir, Petite Sirah and Zinfandel. In addition, the winery makes Burgundy and Chablis.

For a young winery, Kenwood Vineyards has shown remarkable success with emphasis on quality.

Mark West Vineyards

Mark West Vineyards is located on the Trenton-Healdsburg Road near Forestville, about one mile east of the Russian River. The 116-acre former dairy farm was discovered by Bob and Joan Ellis in their search for a new life style.

Dissatisfied with the rapid increase in population and the subsequent changes taking place in the once rural town of Alamo, they yearned for a change. After investigating the possibilities from New Mexico to Washington, their interest in wine and their attraction to Sonoma County led them to the old dairy farm in 1973.

Studies and tests of soil and climate conditions confirmed their initial beliefs and reactions to the farm. Not only did the land fulfill their requirements of having a view, privacy, and trees; but it also was ideally suited to the planting of their four favorite varietals: Pinot Noir, Chardonnay, Gewurztraminer, and Johannisberg Riesling. The area's long growing period (Region I classification) combined with the cool nights produce some excellent sugar-acid ratios in these early maturing varieties.

Bob Ellis is a pilot for Pan Am, but while continuing to fly eleven to twelve days a month, he joined Joan in several enology courses at Davis and helped in the planting of 62½ acres of vines. His subsequent enrollment in several viticulture classes at Santa Rosa Junior College defined his responsibility in the vineyards while Joan has her hands full in the lab and winery.

The Ellis' celebrated their first crush in 1976 inside the original milking barn. It was but one of several outbuildings surrounding their 1903 farmhouse and served adequately for the production of 1400 cases. Beginning with the 1977 crush, their modern equipment and new cooperage will be housed in a new winery.

Construction of the 3500 square foot winery building was begun in June, 1977. Under the able direction of builder, Ron Luddy, the main portion was raised after remodeling work on the existing milking barn. The result was a homogeneous unit, incorporating the old structure as lab and office facilities. The redwood frame construction has been designed to stay cool naturally with the use of polyurethane insulation. The design allows for further addition since the Ellis' intend to plant another 25 acres in vines.

The concept of total control is a big advantage for this new winery. Bob terms it an "Estate Winery" - in one restricted area they live, run a vineyard, operate a winery, and even maintain a greenhouse where vines for their second planting were raised. With the help of consultant, Lawrence Wara, they hope to reach their projected maximum production of 15,000 cases around 1982.

In spite of their busy schedules, the Ellis' will arrange for visits from dedicated wine enthusiasts.

Joseph Swan Vineyards

1973
Sonoma

Estate **Pinot Noir** Bottled

Joseph Swan Vineyards

TABLE WINE 750 ML · (25.4 FL. OZ.)
Produced and Bottled by Joseph Swan Vineyards, Forestville, California

On the outskirts of Forestville near the Lagoon of the Roses is Joseph Swan Vineyards. It is situated at the intersection of Laguna and Trenton Roads in the heart of a very old grape and apple region.

The 13-acre vineyard estate dates back to 1885 when it was used as headquarters for the town of Trenton. The wood frame house contained all the local services the townspeople needed: a grocery store, a post office and (a little later) a switchboard. In the cellars, many years later, were found several 85-gallon puncheons and 60-gallon casks, which indicated that customers brought their wine jugs to the store to buy their wine.

Although the original owners are unknown, in 1915 the property was acquired by a European family named Entzminger. They maintained vineyards and orchards. In 1967, Joseph Swan purchased the land from Florence Entzminger Bolester, a relative of the family. The Swans use the wood frame residence for their home. Part of the barn houses the labeling and bottling facilities. The winery is located at the back of the property.

When Swan cleared the land, he kept a small plot of 50-year-old Zinfandel vines. In 1968, he made some wine from these grapes for home use. Zinfandel is a type of wine for which he has since become famous. In addition, the acreage was planted with five acres of Chardonnay, five acres of Pinot Noir and one half acre

of Cabernet Sauvignon. Each year, Swan buys between six and eight tons of Zinfandel from a grower in Dry Creek. Annual production of all vintaged varieties will run from 1200 to 1500 cases of Chardonnay, Pinot Noir and Zinfandel.

Swan Vineyards is located in a small, cool microclimate with air currents from Bodega Bay to the south and Russian River to the north. The fog which comes in from the ocean maintains added moisture during the growing season.

"The Chardonnay will do as well here as anywhere in California. Only time will tell on the Pinot Noir," says Swan.

Swan's inspiration for winemaking originated during his boyhood reading experiences in Minnesota. Entranced by the romantic and beautiful descriptions of wine, he experimented with a brew of rhubarb wine. Unbeknownst to his teetotler parents, he used the upstairs attic and chicken coop for his concoctions. Years later, while a pilot for Western Airlines, Swan dabbled with an experimental plot of varietals located at 5,000 feet in the Sierra Nevada. The Chardonnay and Pinot Noir vines excelled all other varieties without a trace of frost damage.

The winemaking procedure follows classical methods with emphasis on proper aging. The Zinfandel ages two years in 60-gallon French oak casks and six months in bottle, and the Pinot Noir follows roughly the same process. The Chardonnay sees seven to eight months in wood and three to four months in bottle. Swan believes in minimal handling and cellar treatment. He never filters.

Martini & Prati Wines, Inc.

High on top of Vine Hill in southern Sonoma County is Martini & Prati Wines, Inc. First known as the Lone Fir Vineyard, the business once belonged to Juliette and Joseph Atherton of Oahu, Hawaii, but it has been most closely associated over the years with the Martini name.

Before 1900, Rafaelo Martini from Lucca, Italy, voyaged around the Cape Horn to California. He prospered in agriculture and livestock in the Moss Beach-Princeton area. In 1902, he bought vineyards in Sonoma.

In 1910, son Narcisco Martini with some help from his five brothers bought out their father. They cleared more land and added other varietals, such as Zinfandel, to enlarge their line of bulk wines. The winery was the second largest firm in Sonoma County and it managed to function through Prohibition by making sacramental wines.

By 1943, the Martini property was sold to W.A. Taylor & Co., a subsidiary of the larger Hiram Walker & Co. Elmo Martini (now the oldest surviving family member) became manager of the former family operation and five other wineries in the Bay Area.

In 1951, Elmo Martini and Enrico Prati joined forces. They bought back the winery from Taylor and in the process created a historic merger of two noted California wine families. Prati had gained his professional experience first as a foreman then later as an owner of

Italian Swiss Colony. However, less than a year passed before Prati died and his son Edward assumed his position. Today, the winery is run by Elmo Martini, his two sons, Jim and Tom, and Edward (Pete) Prati, Jr.

Just off Laguna Road stands the winery landmark, a silver watertower which spells the winery's name in big, black letters. The ancient farmhouse sits behind the white, green-trimmed winery. The latter has seven gables and an overhanging ranch-style roofline.

"These two rows of 8,000 and 9,000 gallon redwood tanks, which I have moved three different times, were handmade around 1900," points out Martini. "They were lumbered at Guerneville and made expressly for the Trenton Winery (one of the old wineries in the area long since torn down).

The grapes are grown on the Martini farm and the Prati farm. The grapes consist of seven types of red and six types of white. Additional grapes are purchased from local growers. Martini and Prati sell the majority of their wine in bulk to Paul Masson and Gallo, but there is considerable production under the company label.

"At Martini & Prati, we make our wines in the Italian style. As with any winery, there are certain cellar characteristics or ways of treatment which are unique. As an example we make extensive use of redwood," says Martini.

As originally, the winery has been run primarily as a bulk operation with some interest in producing private labels for selected customers. Within the last 25 years, Martini & Prati put out a selection of dry table wines under their own label.

Russian River Vineyards

The tall wooden towers at the winery at Russian River Vineyards dominate the Forestville landscape. The architecture of the winery was inspired by two distinct and separate Sonoma structures: the hop kiln and Ft. Ross. The hop kiln is an agricultural landmark seen throughout the county. Ft. Ross was the stockade built by the Russian settlers when they established their northern California outpost.

In 1969, Robert Lasden, a former home winemaker, founded the winery. He developed his interest in commercial winemaking sufficiently enough to build a winery and plant vineyards on a 30 acre ranch in Forestville. In 1975, Russian River Vineyards was purchased by two San Franciscans, Jack Lowe and Roy Georgi Jr., who are involved professionally in real estate development.

The winery, which was designed by Lasden, is built of pre-stressed concrete and redwood. The area in front of the winery was made into a brick patio. Below the winery is a century old, brown-shingle building which houses the tasting and sales room as well as a restaurant. The restaurant features continental cuisine and is open for brunch and dinner.

Russian River Vineyards had approximately 27 acres of gently sloping vineyard. The vines rest on the site of an ancient Pomo Indian village. Rare Indian artifacts and relics such as arrowheads and pottery have been discovered during planting and cultivation. The acreage is divided into 12 acres of Chardonnay, 12 acres of Cabernet Sauvignon and three acres of Merlot. Any wine grapes which the winery does not grow in their vineyards are purchased from vineyards within seven miles of the winery.

The vineyard is four miles from the Russian River which in part accounts for it being alternately locked in fog or drenched in sunshine during the growing season.

While in the past Russian River Vineyards has produced a long list of Sonoma County wines, the new winery management will narrow its emphasis to several top, premium varietals. The wines selected for specialization are Chardonnay, Cabernet Sauvignon, Petite Sirah and Zinfandel. The wines are estate-bottled and vintage-dated. The winery will also make two generic wines, a Burgundy and a Chablis.

"At present the new owners are trying to determine the most promising course for their business," explains winemaker Larry Henzerting. "The plans are to make four premium varietals which will be supported by our generics, available in one and a half litre and three litre sizes. Our total output will be in the vicinity of 5,000 cases annually. In the far future, the winery will expand to around 20,000 cases."

One of the only wineries to have a gourmet restaurant on the premises, the quaint European-style eatery is run by talented chef Udo Lukens. Featuring continental cuisine, the restaurant is opened for dinner Thursday through Sunday, 6 p.m. to 10 p.m. and for Sunday brunch 10 a.m. to 2 p.m. The Russian River Vineyards' wines comprise the list.

F. Korbel & Bros.

The red-brick, ivy laden Korbel Champagne Cellars overlook the banks of the Russian River in Guerneville (pronounced "Gurnville"). Slowly built, almost brick by brick, over a period of decades, the winery represents the adventures and achievements of its industrious Czechoslovakian founders the three Korbel brothers. Joseph was a gunsmith, Anton was a locksmith and Francis was a cigarmaker.

The Korbels left Prague in 1850 and sailed to San Francisco on a clipper ship. When they landed, they found a burgeoning boomtown in need of skilled trades people. Demand for the raw materials for cigars and boxes led them to journey to the luxuriant redwood forests on the Russian River.

Once they reached their destination, Stumptown, which later became Guerneville, they bought nearly 6,000 acres of land for prices as reasonable as 35 cents an acre. The virgin timber was lumbered and processed in the Korbel sawmill.

After the lumber was depleted, the trio tried to raise tobacco (for cigars), olives and dairy cows. Their efforts were unsuccessful. It wasn't until they grew European grape varieties that they realized the potential of the land. No less than redwoods, grapes seemed to thrive in the foggy, damp coastal climate, and Guerneville was only 12 miles from Jenner where the Russian River dumps into the Pacific Ocean.

When the Korbels harvested their grapes, the going price were a mere $3.50 a ton. Rather than sell grapes at a loss, they made wine in the back barn. Thus, by the early 1860's this great wine legacy was founded.

In 1886, the original winery building, which still stands, was completed. For three decades the family interest centered on winemaking, but in 1899 a Norman tower was added at the back of the winery to house a copper still, thus production expanded into brandymaking.

By the turn-of-the-century San Francisco was in its heyday as the entertainment capital of the west. As a result, repeated requests for champagne influenced the family to send to Czechoslovakia for Frank Hasak, a champagne master. As popularity of wine and brandy slackened, champagne came even more into vogue, and Korbel became one of America's most respected champagne producers.

In 1954, descendants of the original founders sold their winery to Adolph and Paul Heck. The descendants' prime concern was that the new owners would maintain the quality of the wine establishment. The reputation of the Heck family, from the St. Louis firm of Cook's Imperial Champagne, was pledged to meet their requirements.

Since their takeover of the business in the fifties, the Hecks have put new energy into an increasingly successful operation. They have created a more modern champagne production and aging facility. New buildings constructed include a wine bottling and shipping warehouse, a champagne fermenting area and a crush-

The Old Brandy Distillery at Korbel

ing plant.

The long-term management emphasis has been directed toward strengthening and upgrading of champagne, wine and brandy lines.

"Korbel sells 70 percent of its wine out of state and 30 percent in California," says Gary Heck, vice president of sales and finance and son of Adolph. "Champagne leads sales of brandy, then comes wine."

Korbel farms 600 acres of wine grapes, the majority of which are adjacent to the Russian River, the balance of which are within a radius of 20 miles. The wet, rain-forest atmosphere in the winter combined with the warm, dry summer still produces unusually good quality grapes, as the Korbel brothers discovered a century ago.

Korbel makes champagne in the classical French "methode champenoise," which requires secondary fermentation in the bottle. The primary fermentation duplicates the customary procedure for still wines. In the spring Adolph Heck, champagne master, creates the cuvee' or blend which is often composed of different vintages and varieties. Yeast and sugar cane are added to the cuvee. Bottles are filled with wine and then the secondary cold-fermentation may begin. During this period, a special, continually cultured yeast, first brought from Germany in 1944, converts sugar into alcohol and carbon dioxide. Net result when the cork is pulled are the bubbles that release the unique champagne flavor. Korbel allows the champagne to age on the yeast for approximately two years before it is placed on motorized riddling racks. These racks shake the yeast down the side of the bottle to the neck. A portion of the wine is then poured off or disgorged, a process which allows the sediment to escape. The lost wine is replaced and the sugar is added. After re-corking the wine and securing it with a wire hood, the bottle is labeled and laid away for several more months before it is time to go to the marketplace. The most popular champagnes nationally are Brut, Extra Dry, Natural, Sec, Rose' and Rouge.

"I am still learning," says Adolph Heck, president and chairman of the Korbel board. "Even after 40 years of champagne-making, I have found without question, it is better to make champagne the hard way in the bottle as they do in Europe. There is no short cut for quality." He refers here to the traditional French method of individual bottle fermentation, as opposed to the "bulk" method employed by many wineries who make domestically produced champagne.

In addition, Korbel continues to develop its interest in still wine. By 1980, the winery's vintage-dated, estate-bottled selection will include Chardonnay, Johannisberg Riesling, Chenin Blanc, Gewurztraminer, Grey Riesling, Sonoma Blanc (Sauvignon Blanc), Cabernet Sauvignon, Pinot Noir and Zinfandel. The winery also makes Burgundy, Chablis and Rose'.

All the red wines are fermented in stainless steel fermenters which have an outside cooling sleeve to control fermentation temperatures. For the most part the reds are aged two to three years in 2,000 gallon eastern oak barrels and finished in smaller 50 gallon American white oak barrels. The reds are all bottle-aged.

The whites are fermented in stainless steel. The Chardonnay is the one exception, and has a touch of oak.

Davis Bynum Winery

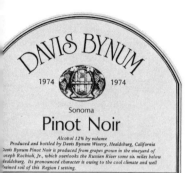

In 1964 Davis Bynum made a major decision which changed his life. He left his job as a reporter for the San Francisco Chronicle and became a winemaker. One year later, in 1965, he founded and opened the Davis Bynum Winery in Albany, California, not far from the campus of the University of California in Berkeley.

Bynum began by buying bulk wine which he blended and bottled under his own label. In 1971, he purchased a 25-acre vineyard in the Napa Valley from which he obtained grapes for winemaking at the Albany Winery. The winery gained public attention for its whimsical Barefoot Bynum label, fondly called the Chateau La Feet of California, its Mead, wine made from honey and its Davis Bynum line of dry table wines.

In 1973, as business improved, the Davis Bynum Winery, Inc., was formed and purchased the 82-acre River Bend ranch near the Russian River in Healdsburg. The Albany Winery remained an active center for winemaking.

The property was formerly the site of a hops ranch whose beginnings dated to the early 1900's. In 1949, the first hop kiln had burned to the ground but was reconstructed soon after. This second hop kiln is the present day winery.

As an individual, Davis Bynum is a very warm and genuine person. A fourth generation Californian, he was greatly influenced by his father, Lindley Bynum, a historian and wine judge, who wrote *California Wines and How to Enjoy Them.* Today Bynum has been successful in fulfilling his desire to grow grapes and make wine in Sonoma County.

Approximately 85 per cent of the winery's grapes are grown in vineyards along or near Westside Road in Healdsburg. The corporation owns 20 acres of Pinot Noir and 25 acres of Chardonnay. The vineyards are planted on the side of a hill with southeastern exposure. The presence of the Russian River accounts for cooler weather and some fog which results in the grapes taking a longer time to ripen.

Our concept is to concentrate on Sonoma County," explains Bynum with a smile. "We want to define specific areas in which grapes can be grown such as Zinfandel from the Dry Creek Valley or Westside Rd."

As winemaker Bynum believes in making and holding the majority of his white wines in stainless steel, and this results in wines with a young, fresh character. The Chardonnay is the one exception; it is aged in wood and bottle. In contrast, the red wines are aged in a combination of French, American and Yugoslavian oak with additional time in bottle.

In the new tasting room which has opened on Solano Ave. in Albany (the old facility is licensed for the production of Mead only) one may taste a variety of vintage-dated table wines. The wines include Chardonnay, White Riesling, French Colombard, Sauvignon Blanc, Cabernet Sauvignon, Petite Sirah, Pinot Noir, Zinfandel and Merlot. Current annual production runs 15,000 cases, but future projections show production of 20,000.

Hop Kiln Winery

The imposing stone and redwood-turreted Hop Kiln Winery is a historic site of Griffin Vineyards. It is found at the bend of Westside Road just beyond the turnoff to Sweetwater Springs Road.

In 1960 the property was bought by Dr. L. Martin Griffin Jr., and the winery was established in 1975. Originally, the 380-acre Sweetwater Springs Ranch (as it was once called) belonged to Solomon Walters. Oldtimers say it is one of the oldest settlements in the Healdsburg area, dating back to the early 1800's. It is located along the Russian River on the southern boundary line of the historic Rancho Sotoyome land grant. On the grounds there can still be seen a Victorian house, an 1880's sheep barn, a lambing shed, a wash house, a machine shop, cottages and the Hop Kiln Winery.

In its heyday, the Sweetwater Springs Ranch was known for its large-scale hop production a key ingredient used in making beer. A fine example of architecture and a tribute to Sonoma's agricultural past, the hop kiln has been converted into a winery and museum. It was built at the turn-of-the-century by 25 men in 35 days, Angelo Sodini a member of the crew, whose name is also associated with the construction of Jack London's Wolf House, Soda Rock Winery and Simi Winery.

As a visit to the winery quickly confirms, the emphasis at Hop Kiln Winery is on the maintenance of agricultural values. Since his acquisition of the ranch and hop kiln, Dr. Griffin has restored the ridge pole connecting the two sections of the barn and rebuilt the fallen tower. He has left standing the furnace and the two-story hop press so that visitors can learn about hops as well as wine. Outside there are other reminders of the hop-growing past.

From the upper deck of the hop kiln winery, one can see the 65 acres of vineyards which are planted along the Russian River, and on the surrounding hillsides. Griffin has found the climate excellent for growing wine grapes. The area is usually cool due to its proximity to the Pacific Ocean and the influence of the coastal fog. The fog recedes by mid-morning; in the afternoon, the hot sun brings warm weather which is good for ripening grapes in the late summer.

The winery makes vintage-dated, estate-bottled varietal wines. The wines are Petite Sirah, Zinfandel, Gamay Beaujolais, Johannisberg Riesling and French Colombard. The label displays a hop kiln on the front and a griffin, a mythological beast, on the side.

Dr. Griffin learned winemaking while he was living in Florence, Italy. In his spare time, he visited the wineries in the Chianti countryside.

"As a winemaker, I let the seasons do the work for me. I let the cold winter do the precipitating and fining. I keep the winery cold. If I want heat stabilization, I let the reds and whites set through the summer. I let wine clear up naturally with minimal mechanical interference," explains Dr. Griffin.

Hop Kiln Winery plans its production to remain small—at about 4500 cases a year.

Mill Creek Winery

Overlooking the scenic Dry Creek and Russian River valleys is one of the newest of the Sonoma County wineries —Mill Creek Vineyards. From its secluded hillside spot, the winery offers a magnificent view of the wine country, the kaleidoscope of vineyard colors offset by the purplish haze of Mount St. Helena in the distance.

Although the winery is brand new, it is the realization of a plan begun 11 years ago by Charles Kreck, a patient but determined native Californian whose goal of producing fine 100% varietal wines from his own mature grapes is slowly being achieved.

After moving his family from Los Angeles to Healdsburg in 1949, Chuck Kreck became involved in ranching. As his love of California wine and the Sonoma County wine country grew, Chuck began searching for the land best suited to his four favorite wines: Cabernet Sauvignon, Chardonnay, Pinot Noir, and Merlot. Following extensive research involving tests of soil and climate conditions, he finally selected 75 acres situated on the alluvial fan formed by Dry Creek.

From 1965 to 1972 Chuck and his two sons worked to turn prune orchards into vineyards. Now in 1976, the vines are mature enough to begin production of their own estate-bottled wines.

Mill Creek Vineyards is a family-owned and operated winery in the purest sense: all aspects of the winery operation are controlled by family members. Chuck is the founder and supervisor of the enterprise, with his wife Vera adding her support and her willingness to fill in anywhere she's needed—from working on the bottling line to greeting visitors. Son Bill is the vineyard and sales manager and with his wife Yvonne supervises the public relations aspect of the venture. Chuck's other son Bob is studying enology and currently assists Robert Stemmler, wine consultant, in the winemaking responsibilities at Mill Creek. Bob plans to assume the role of winemaker in the near future. Bob's wife Licia is the winery's office manager, performing the essential bookkeeping and secretarial functions, and, of course, all the Krecks participate in tasting and judging their wines.

The winery itself is a functional building, 6200 square feet of cement block. Inside are rows of new American and French oak cooperage sharing space with American and Yugoslavian oak tanks and the most modern winery equipment available. A separate tasting room and extended picnic grounds will be added.

With their vineyards in close proximity to the winery, crushing can begin within minutes of harvesting, distinctly aiding the production of top quality wines. As Bill Kreck comments, ''The advantage here at Mill Creek is that we can strictly control all phases of winemaking, from the planting of the grapes to the bottling of the wine. There is a feeling of continuity and of shared goals.'' It is the consensus of the family that an upper limit of 10,000 cases per year be set in order to keep the winery small enough to produce only wines of optimum quality.

119

Landmark Vineyards

LANDMARK

SONOMA VALLEY

CHARDONNAY
1974

Alcohol 13.4% by volume

Produced and Bottled by the Cellars of Landmark Vineyards, Napa, California

An avenue of tall, stately cypresses leads past the Spanish hacienda and under a portico to Landmark Winery. A hint of Landmark's future existence came in 1970, when William R. Mabry Jr., a retired Air Force officer and architect, and his son began farming in Vineburg, near Sonoma. The operation was expanded with the addition of vineyards in Alexander Valley. Another facility handled Landmark's first crushes in 1974 and 1975. Their own winery was begun in Windsor in September of 1975.

Originally from Sonoma, Mabry was familiar with the grape industry of the county; he and his family prepared themselves for the venture for many years. The Windsor location, one of several properties evaluated, was selected for its Class I soil, a suitable climate for white wine grapes, and its easy access for customers. In the '20s and '30s the estate had been a model prune operation, with orchards and prune dryers.

Known locally as "The Hembree Place," it had been the home of the popular and well known physician Dr. Atlas Hembree. The original, now tilting farmhouse, whose roof sprouts kelly green moss, will be restored as a retail outlet. The mansion, built in the late 1920s, houses the tasting room and offices. Well-maintained gardens surround the main buildings and several shaded paths wind past angular reflecting ponds, wooded glens, and a meandering waterway.

The estate was purchased from unsuccessful gubernatorial candidate William Matson Roth, owner of Matson Steamship Lines. Unfortunately, completion of Highway 101 had divided the property, influencing Roth's decision to sell. The Mabrys will gradually phase out the 55 acres of prune orchards as their vineyards are expanded. The remaining acreage has already been planted to Johannisberg Riesling, Gewurztraminer, and Chardonnay.

The new winery is of traditional Spanish architecture, with stucco walls, shake roof, and arched redwood doors. William Mabry Jr. designed the building and his son, William Mabry III, also a partner, was in charge of construction.

Landmark produces 3000 cases a year and may eventually reach 25,000 cases annually. Featuring only vintaged Sonoma County wines, production includes the whites listed above, Pinot Noir, and Cabernet Sauvignon.

Most of the red varieties are planted in the Alexander Valley, one of the warmest spots in the county. The vineyards roll down a hillside and onto the valley floor and produce excellent sugar/acid ratios. The whites will come from the Mabrys' Windsor and Vineburg locations.

Landmark is a family concern. William Mabry Jr. handles financing and general management duties; his wife, Maxine, heads marketing. William Mabry III runs the operations of the winery and his wife, Michele, is office manager and bookkeeper. R. Brad Webb is consulting enologist.

Sonoma Vineyards

It all began in 1959 in a yellow, two-story, wood-frame house on Main St. in Tiburon, California. After working as a wine apprentice in both Europe and California, former dancer and choreographer, Rodney D. Strong, decided to open his own small, retail wine shop.

The Tiburon Vintners (as it originally was called) wine concept was simple enough, but could it work: wine purchased in bulk, bottled in fifths and sold by direct mail or retail? The Tiburon residence was modeled after a European arrangement. Living quarters were upstairs; wine shop was downstairs; and the makeshift winery was in the cellar. The modest guestbook, regularly kept, became the backbone of a multi-million-dollar direct mail wine business.

As consumer enthusiasm grew and personalized labels became vogue, Strong sensed a need for his own winery and vineyards. In 1962, he bought the 1898 Windsor Winery from wine merchant Fred Perry, who had done business under the Monte Carlo label.

"Business was successful," remarks Strong, now vice president and winemaster for Sonoma Vineyards. "It was direct to the consumer at reasonable rates, door to door."

In 1964, Peter Freidman, a New Yorker, joined the organization and became a partner. Business continued to flourish and Windsor Winery, with its 50,000 case production capacity could not satisfy demand. Plans were made to construct a modern California wine center and utilize the best in modern equipment and scientific technology.

Change came quickly. Nearly 650 acres adjacent to the Windsor property were acquired and planted. Today the winery owns nearly 2,000 acres of land, but no additional acreage has been planted. For the winery, architect Greg Knowland designed a twentieth century structure with four rectangles extending from a central axis. From the air it simulates a maltese cross; from eye level it rises at a bold angle thrusting sharply to the sky. It is made of Russian River stone and redwood.

By 1973, Sonoma Vineyards was officially opened. The physical layout of the plant covers 160,000 square feet. The winery is equipped with 52 stainless steel jacketed fermenters and an extensive array of related equipment. It has one million gallons of fermentation capacity and 3.5 million gallons storage capacity, one million gallons is Slavonian and French oak cooperage and 2.5 million gallons is stainless steel. In 1975, the winery produced 250,000 cases.

"Today we are looking at the national market," states Strong. We strive to be a premium winery and specialize in Chardonnay, Johannisberg Riesling, Cabernet Sauvignon and Pinot Noir. We want to grow all our varietals as vineyard-designated, estate-bottled vintaged wines."

Following a financial reorganization in 1976, Renfield Importers, Ltd., of New York City acquired an equity interest and became sole national distributors of Sonoma Vineyards.

Foppiano Vineyards

Foppiano Vineyards parallels the Russian River for a mile along the river's eastern border just south of Healdsburg. Low-lying hills, once the burial grounds of Central Pomo Indians, surround the almost perfectly square 200-acre parcel.

Lured by the talk of riches in the far western United States, enterprising John Foppiano bade farewell to Genoa, Italy, and headed for the gold mines in Sonora, California. Although Foppiano did not find the precious metal in the gold country, he did discover the great fertile agricultural preserve along the Russian River. For a period, he raised vegetables. But, common sense and his winemaking instincts told him there was greater opportunity in other endeavors. In 1896, he bought a 100-acre working winery and residence, which was part of the original Mexican land grant Rancho Sotoyome. In that same year, he founded the Foppiano Wine Co.

Earlier, in 1858, the old home had been called the Riverside Inn. It was then an hospitable overnight lodge for stagecoach passengers traveling the Old Redwood Highway and for train passengers riding the Northwestern Pacific Railroad.

In the early days, the emphasis at the winery was on cooperation and hard work. Everyone joined the labors from dawn to dusk. By 1910, son Louis Andrew Foppiano was in a position to buy the bulk winery from his father. Following his death in 1924 and an accommodation to Prohibition, son Louis Joseph Foppiano and his widow, Mathilda Foppiano, rebuilt the winery from top to bottom.

Since that time, the winery building has remained much the same with the exception of a green exterior paint job. The interior speaks of both the past and the present. The high wooden ceilings leave ample room for the huge old redwood tanks and the newer shiny, stainless steel jacketed fermenters stand nearby.

The ancient farmhouse where Louis Foppiano was born is now used as the business office and retail tasting room. He has given more and more responsibility to his sons: Lou Foppiano Jr., head of sales and production and Rod Foppiano, chief of viticulture.

Foppiano Winery produces close to 150,000 cases a year with a million gallon storage capacity. One quarter of the production is in varietals; three-fourths is devoted to generics. The interest in varietals has produced a selection of estate-bottled, vintage-dated premium table wines which include Zinfandel, Cabernet Sauvignon, Pinot Noir, Petite Sirrah, French Colombard and Sonoma Fume.

The Russian River plays an important part in the life of the winery. The river brings in a low fog which adds moisture to the air and has a beneficial effect on the growth cycle. Vines thrust deep into the gravelly benchland which was once riverbed. The gravelly sand makes the ground permeable to a great depth, allows rain to pass through it and encourages the vine to find rich food sources. Because of the nearness of the river, the overall climate tends to be warm, with some inland breezes.

Sotoyome Winery

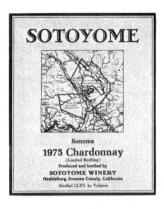

The map on this new wine label pinpoints Sotoyome Winery in the southern sector of the Rancho Sotoyome land grant. The most credible explanation of the origin of the name Sotoyome was handed down from Mrs. Henry D. Fitch, widowed wife of the custodian of the land grant and sister-in-law of General Vallejo. She said it meant "village of brave warriors," referring to the tribe of Indians that inhabited the Russian River Valley.

The road to the Sotoyome Winery passes through back country roads, over a railroad trestle and up a steep driveway just off Limerick Lane. The hillside hideaway, composed of the subtle yellow winery and modern redwood house, sits on the crest of the ridge. There is a 360 degree panorama.

One side the view looks toward Fitch Mountain, Cambiaso Winery and the silhouetted Adam and Eve redwood grove. On the other side the pastoral vista faces 40-year-old Zinfandel vines and Andrew Sodoni's old Italian winery.

In 1973, William Chaikin, a Los Angeles manufacturer and native of California, and John C. Stampfl, a 30-year-veteran-winemaker and graduate of UC Davis, collaborated with other investors to form a small, do-it-yourself wine enterprise.

After extensive explorations, the group decided on the greater Healdsburg wine district. Their choice centered on a 100-year-old wine making and grape growing business. Italian and French families had planted and harvested the region for decades, --why shouldn't they continue. The end result was purchase of a piece of land which had formerly belonged to Anacleto Ricci, a prosperous Italian fruit grower. He specialized in apples, prunes and grapes.

Eight acres of Zinfandel vines surrounding the winery and seven acres of Chardonnay and Cabernet from the Dry Creek area provide the basis of the grape supply. The remainder come from sources in sight of the residence.

During prime growing time, the mornings are frequently foggy with a slow accumulation of daytime, hillside heat. In the flat of the valley, high temperatures are reached by mid-morning. The combination of the ever-changing Russian River watercourse and natural earthquake faults has produced a mixed soil. Grapes grown under these conditions are high in acid with good color and plenty of sugar.

"Our aim is to use a natural means of wine-making with as little manipulation and complication as possible. Our emphasis is on the best grapes. Our technique is to allow the wine to develop fully. We are more tied to the vintage than to temperature controls, which are most elementary," say Chaikin.

With a capacity of 4,000 cases a year, the owners are using equipment most adaptable to their size. The winery produces three commercial wines: Chardonnay, Cabernet and Zinfandel. All the wines are stored in the fibre glass tanks with some exposure to redwood and smaller American white oak barrels.

Cambiaso Winery and Vineyards

Cambiaso Winery & Vineyards rests in the hills to the southeast of Healdsburg above the Russian River. The area resembles the Italian wine country and the homeland of the winery's founder, Giovanni Cambiaso.

In 1922, Maria and Giovanni Cambiaso left San Francisco for the warmer Sonoma climate. They worked on other people's ranches until they had earned enough money to buy a 52-acre hillside ranch. Initially they had cleared the land of the native fieldstone and used it to build a New England style retaining wall which surrounds the wood-frame house and A-shaped barn. The 35 acres of vineyard were hand-planted with mixed varieties.

From the beginning Cambiaso Winery developed a friendly style of service. The customer was always placed first. Originally capital was raised from the sale of grapes direct to neighbors, ranchers and home winemakers. In 1934, the winery was bonded. Commercial wines were made in 1000 gallon redwood tanks and sold in 50 gallon barrels to restaurants, grocery stores and home-users. Always determined and strong-willed, Giovanni managed to harvest the grapes and make the wine, which he sold and delivered as well.

Cambiaso Winery has always been a family operation. The Cambiasos had three children: Rita, Theresa and Joseph. They all grew up on the ranch and took an active interest in all phases of grape growing and wine production. As their parents grew older, Rita became manager and Joseph, who learned the art from his father, became winemaker. Until then, the winery was solely a bulk concern. In the fifties, as the younger generation took over, Cambiaso Winery released several generics under their own label. It wasn't until 1972 that the winery bottled and labeled varietals.

"Our philosophy has always been to make clean, simple wine," declares Rita Cambiaso, who still manages the business.

In 1972, Cambiaso Winery was purchased by a group of business men from Thailand from the Four Seas Corporation. Rita Cambiaso has stayed on and Joseph Cambiaso remains as winemaker. Since the change of ownership, the winery has expanded its capacity from 150,000 gallons to 750,000 gallons a year. The quality remains high.

The place where recent physical change appears most apparent is the wine plant. The original wood winery seems antiquated next to the big, modern steel and concrete winery. It houses new stainless steel fermenting tanks. The new case storage area is virtually the size of a football field.

Through the years, Cambiaso Winery has developed a very strong connection with the restaurant trade. It is not unusual to find the products on the wine lists of restaurants throughout the greater San Francisco area. Cambiaso wines are available in some retail wine shops. In addition the winery also produces some private labels, with an annual production of some 80,000 cases.

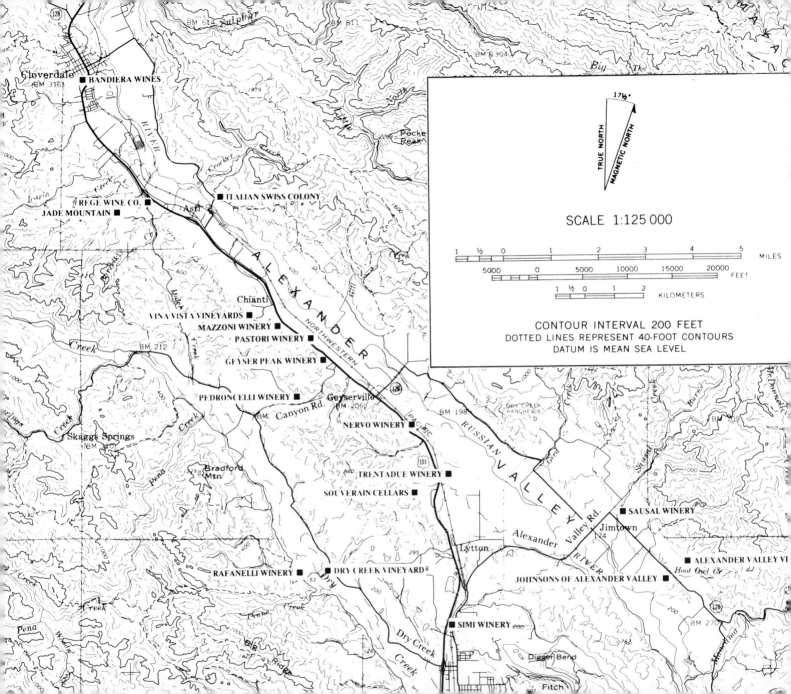

SCALE 1:125 000

CONTOUR INTERVAL 200 FEET
DOTTED LINES REPRESENT 40-FOOT CONTOURS
DATUM IS MEAN SEA LEVEL

Northern Sonoma Wineries

Alexander Valley Vineyards

Alexander Valley Vineyards is situated in one of the most picturesque settings in all the Sonoma wine country. A white Victorian mansion sits on a hill, nestled against a mountain of greenery and surrounded by trellised vineyards.

During the late fifties and early sixties, the family of Harry Wetzel Jr., an executive of the Los Angeles-based Garret Corporation, frequently visited Russell Green, a one-time owner of Simi Winery. Wetzel's visits to the Alexander Valley whetted his interest in grape growing and winemaking. In 1963, he bought the ranch of Cyrus Alexander, caretaker of the Rancho Sotoyome land grant for Gen. Mariano Vallejo, from the descendants of Alexander.

It was in 1849 that Cyrus and Raffina Alexander built and occupied the first adobe house in Sonoma County. They raised and sold vegetables to gold miners heading for the California gold fields as their principal means of support. Over the years, the Alexander ranch was leased for grazing sheep and cattle. In the 1960's, it was converted into vineyards.

The stately Victorian residence, where the Wetzels now live, rests on a knoll overlooking the valley. The house has been renovated and improved. The grounds are professionally landscaped and manicured. There are fig, quince, apple and persimmon trees. In the courtyard one can find a circular pond and fruit and vegetable gardens. Walking over a foot bridge and up a hill one comes upon the remodeled 1886 Victorian Alexander Valley schoolhouse. On another hill behind the winery lies the Alexander family graveyard now hidden in tall grasses and over a century of memories.

In 1975, Wetzel began construction on the Spanish-American slumpstone and redwood winery. It has a tasting room, offices above the vineyard, balconies, a fermentation area and a two-story wine cellar. The winery is equipped with modern 3,000 gallon stainless steel jacketed fermenters and four 1500-gallon stainless storage tanks. Some of the white wines are held in stainless steel. The red wine is aged in a combination of 60-gallon French Limousin oak barrels and 50-gallon American white oak casks.

Alexander Valley Vineyards is controlled by a partnership which includes Harry Wetzel Jr., and his son Harry (Hank) Wetzel III, and Daler Goode, vineyard manager. The 250 acres of vineyards in front of the winery are owned by Harry Wetzel Jr. and Russell Green. The vineyards are made up of Cabernet Sauvignon, Pinot Noir, Zinfandel, Merlot, Chardonnay, Johannisberg Riesling, Gewurztraminer and Chenin Blanc.

"We are trying to make dry table wines which combine production of modern technique with lessons of the traditional past. I learned winemaking from Jerry Luper and Bradford Webb at Freemark Abbey in St. Helena," recalls Harry Wetzel III, winemaker.

The 7,000 case-a-year winery makes three vintage-dated, estate-bottled table wines whose label notes the Alexander Valley area of origin. The wines are Chardonnay, Johannisberg Riesling and Cabernet.

Johnsons' of Alexander Valley

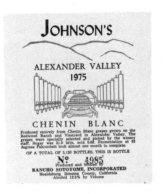

Three brothers, Tom, Will and Jay Johnson, are co-proprietors of the newly established Johnsons' of Alexander Valley. Founded in 1975, it is located on the Rancho Soto-yome land grant near the Russian River in Healdsburg. The land was obtained by their father James Johnson, a San Francisco lawyer, in 1952.

The property's history as an active winery dates back to the late 1800's. Wine was then distributed in barrels, transported by horse-drawn wagon to the old Lytton train station (now dismantled) and shipped via railroad to points south. The ranch house (still intact) remains a unique example of California architecture. Containing no studs or frame, it was constructed of horizontal redwood boards outside and vertical redwood boards inside. Square and without ornamentation, it resembles a cardboard box. The winery was a simple wooden building.

During its heyday, the 150-acre ranch supported a healthy crop of prunes, pears and grapes. In the late fifties, when the price of grapes fell to the lowest in a decade and the prunes were plagued by an incurable root disease, the Johnsons experienced hard times financially. By 1966, however, conditions had improved and new varietal vineyards supplanted the prune orchards.

In 1972, the three brothers pooled their resources and bought the ranch from their father. They decided to sell grapes and pears commercially until their winery got underway.

Retaining the rustic character of the wooden barn, they remodeled the interior with equipment collected on a shoestring budget. From winemaker Joseph Heitz, they obtained a crusher-stemmer and from neighbors James and John Pedroncelli they purchased a press. Most of the cooperage is something less than new.

As a novel attraction, the Johnsons, with the help of friend Bud Kurz, have installed the only Marr & Colton, 30-pipe theatre organ in the Sonoma wine country. Once used as a musical accompaniment for early day silent films, the organ simulates the sounds of several instruments, such as the vibra harp, trumpet, xylophone, calliope, drum and cymbals. In mixed tribute to wine and music, the Johnsons' label is embellished with pipes and theatre organ.

Originally the Johnson boys became interested in winemaking through the encouragement of amateur winemakers who would stop by their farm and buy grapes for their own home winemaking adventures. After some trial and error experimentation, the trio decided that a farm in the Alexander Valley wouldn't be complete without a family-style winery. The first products of the venture became available in 1976.

Tom Johnson, winemaker and vineyard manager, oversees the winemaking process, which is handled very uniformly. All the wines are held in redwood and then transferred into upright Yugoslavian oak and then into smaller American white oak barrels. Available only at the winery, the wines include Pinot Noir, Rose' of Pinot Noir, Chenin Blanc, Zinfandel and Cabernet Sauvignon.

Sausal Winery

A large, twisted juniper graces the entrance to the new Sausal Winery in the Alexander Valley. The smart redwood structure inherits its names from Sausal Creek (meaning willow in Spanish) which meanders through the property to the old quicksilver mine at Pine Flat. Geyser Peak looms in the distance.

The idea for the winery was the dream of the late Leo Demonstene, once the winemaker at Soda Rock Winery, also in the Healdsburg area. In 1950, Demostene became the owner of the 116-acre Sausal Ranch with its abundant grapes, apples and prunes. The ranch was efficiently farmed and over the years improved. Many of the orchards were torn out and replanted with vineyards. A modern brick and wooden house was built on a rise overlooking the property and used as the family residence.

Originally the Demostene family became associated with Soda Rock Winery through Rose Demostene, Leo's widow, who remains a partner in the business with other members of her family. By 1970, the Leo Demostene family decided to end their active involvement at the Soda Rock Winery and go into the wine business at the new location on Sausal Creek. In the spring of 1973, shortly after the death of the father and founder, construction commenced in his honor.

Suddenly the delapidated prune hydrator below the main house was turned into a handsome piece of architecture. Artistically nestled at the foot of the hill, the winery-to-be was done in redwood and equipped with stainless steel fermenters, storage tanks and upright and smaller oak cooperage.

Today Sausal Winery remains a family affair with the children of Leo Demostene at the helm. David Lee Demostene is the enologist, Edward Demostene is vineyard manager, Roselee Demostene is chemist, and (sister) Lucinda Nelson is administrator.

For the most part grapes for the Sausal wines will come from the vineyards surrounding the winery and neighboring family-owned ranches. All of the wines will bear the Alexander Valley designation of origin with the exception of the Dry Creek Zinfandel.

"It takes good grapes to make good wines," says Dave Demostene. "We originally thought we could start out as a good, small bulk producer, but we changed our minds. We will forget quantity and think quality. We have the grapes from this area, the Alexander Valley, so why not?"

The cool, foggy nights and warm, sunny days characteristic of the Alexander Valley are the perfect growing conditions for the line of red wines Sausal is developing. The winery will produce a Burgundy, Zinfandel, Gamay, Petite Sirah and Cabernet Sauvignon. The practice of the winery is to age the wine one to three years with a minimum of six months in bottle. In the future, winery production will not exceed 30,000 cases.

With the blessing of Robert Mondavi, who told David Demostene he was foolish not to bottle under his own label as opposed to sell in bulk, Sausal Winery is off to a great start.

Simi Winery

Simi Winery represents the best of Old World Italy and New World America. In 1848, Pietro and Giuseppe Simi left Tuscany for California. Once there, they laid the foundations for an over 100-year tradition of winemaking. They named their winery Montepulciano in honor of a grape district which lies south of Florence, Italy.

Originally the Simi brothers were vegetable farmers, but their Green Street home in San Francisco soon became known as a combined residence and winery. Grapes were bought in Sonoma, transported by wagon to Petaluma, down the Petaluma River and across the San Francisco Bay by barge and finally delivered to the family home. Gradually the Simis built a reputation in the restaurant trade for producing good wines. Increased sales caused them to look for a more permanent source of grapes in the Sonoma countryside.

In Healdsburg, they founded a 126-acre vineyard. Their first crush took place in a fieldstone winery on Front Street. The foundations still remain. In 1876, the pair built a majestic stone and redwood structure dubbed Montepulciano, Noble Hill.

Unfortunately, the brothers died before the facility was completed. Giuseppe's daughter, Isabelle Simi inherited the winery. Eventually she married Fred Haigh, a local banker, who also shared her interest in the winery. They ran it together to produce bulk wine with some interest in the retail market.

During Prohibition, Simi made sacramental wine, but after Repeal, brandy, port, sherry and champagne were produced. The Hotel Del Monte and Montepulciano labels became fashionable among many Californians. By the fifties, Fred Haigh had died and left Isabelle Haigh at the helm of the historic wine ship.

In 1969, Russell Green, a Los Angeles oilman, bought the winery. He acquired an old name, with old wine, in an old winery. For five years, he re-equipped the winery, established a market and improved the wines. By 1976, Simi Winery was purchased once again, this time by Schieffelin & Co., a New York importing firm. Under the leadership of Michael Dacres Dixon, winery president, prospects for Simi look bright indeed. Mary Ann Graf, one of a handful of women winemakers, continues under the tutelage of consulting enologist Andre Tchelistcheff.

"Winemaking is an art which requires time, intimate time. What I am really looking for in my life is the ideal. It is continually modified by my idea of what the ideal really is. I would like to make the perfect wine. In 10 years, that ideal has changed through tasting, yearly grape changes and by what happens when I do things. If a grape seemingly has potential as the ideal, a person must do the best she can," concludes Miss Graf.

Since the Graf-Tchelistcheff team joined forces, Simi winery has produced some exciting new wines. Together they will work making exclusively nine varietal wines: Chardonnay, Johannisberg Riesling, Chenin Blanc, Rose of Cabernet, Gamay Beaujolais, Zinfandel, Pinot Noir, Cabernet Sauvignon and Gerwurztraminer.

Dry Creek Vineyard

In the heart of Dry Creek Valley at the base of Pine Ridge lies Dry Creek Vineyard. Though a relative newcomer to this historic wine valley, Dry Creek Vineyard already offers an eloquent testimonial to the success of the small winery movement in Sonoma County.

Established in 1973 by ex-suburban Bostonians, Gail and David Stare, the winery and vineyard are on the site of an old ranch.

The idea for the winery originated in the early 1950's during a series of wine tastings held at David Stare's alma mater, Massachusetts Institute of Technology. The Stare's enjoyment of wine led them to cultivate a 40-cutting experimental vineyard obtained from Philip Wagner of Boordy Vineyards in Maryland. Although their first experiments produced only vinegar, their enthusiasm for winemaking was undiminished. In 1967, while working on assignment for a German business firm, the Stares continued to pursue their wine interest. They made friends with German vintners and took trips to the Moselle and Rhinegau.

By 1970, Gail and David had an inkling they would be doing something related to the wine field. For a while they flirted with a French adventure, but common sense brought them closer to home and California. Stare enrolled in U.C. Davis to study enology and viticulture. On spare weekends he traveled the coastal and inland wine areas in search of land. Sonoma even-tually proved to be the place. Land was reasonable, the area's 100 years of successful winemaking had established its quality pattern and the challenge was wide open.

In 1973, the main winery building was constructed and future plans call for adding another wing to be used chiefly for wine storage. Outside the winery building there are 50 acres of Chardonnay, Chenin Blanc, Fume' Blanc and Cabernet Sauvignon grapes. Ideally the Stares would like to be self-sufficient and grow all their own grapes, but until that actually happens they are buying some of their wine grapes from growers in the Healdsburg-Dry Creek area.

From the very beginning, David Stare gained a reputation as a producer of good quality white wines. His Chenin Blanc and Fume' Blanc were quickly and widely accepted. In 1975, he released his first red wines. In reds and whites, his total offering includes vintage-dated Chardonnay, Chenin Blanc, Fume' Blanc, Gamay Beaujolais, Zinfandel, Petite Sirah and Cabernet Sauvignon. The winery is presently producing 12,000 cases per year and plans to slowly grow to a maximum annual production of 20,000 cases.

Dry Creek Vineyard has established a friendly, informative tasting style. Visitors are invited to come into the entrance hall which adjoins the main wine cellar. They are immediately greeted by a knowledgeable host or hostess who encourages their participation in an informal wine discussion. The wine glasses are arranged in a circle on top of a wine barrel. Wines are poured accordingly and sometimes there is the opportunity to compare varieties of different vintages.

Trentadue Winery

Trentadue

SONOMA

Cabernet Sauvignon

PRODUCED AND BOTTLED BY
Trentadue Winery and Vineyards
GEYSERVILLE • SONOMA COUNTY • CALIF.
ALCOHOL 13% BY VOLUME

The Trentadue Winery commands one of the most spectacular views in the upper Alexander Valley. From the vineyards which are located close to the Russian River, one can see both Geyser Peak and Mt. St. Helena.

Although the winery is relatively new, founded in 1969, owners Evelyn and Leo Trentadue are hardly newcomers when it comes to making wine. They descend from a long line of Tuscan winemakers that span several generations. For years, prior to moving to Sonoma County, the Trentadues were involved in agriculture, raising apricots, cherries and prunes in the Santa Clara Valley. On weekends, the family would spend their time at their 50-acre mountain-top retreat at the site of the now defunct Montebello Winery in Cupertino.

Although life was good to the Trentadues, they were influenced to leave Santa Clara County for several reasons. The ever-growing population of the area continually encroached on the countryside causing farmers like Leo Trentadue eventually to sell or subdivide their land for housing. The Trentadues held out longer than many of their neighbors, but eventually decided that there had to be an easier way of farming without the encroaching urbanization.

Meanwhile, for many years, Dick Benion and Paul Draper of the highly regarded Ridge Vineyards had been urging Evelyn and Leo to grow grapes and start a winery on their hilltop Cupertino property. Although the time and place never proved quite right, the twosome's repeated suggestion and encouragement planted the seed for the winery which the Trentadues eventually built in Sonoma County.

In 1959, Trentadue bought two ranches. The Wisecarver Ranch, the largest of the two, consisted of 126 acres, a Victorian mansion, a barn and the Heart's Desire Nursery, which had ties with famed botonist Luther Burbank. Part of the land is now leased to Souverain of the Alexander Valley. Closer to the Russian River lies the other property, the former 42-acre Luchetti Ranch. It had a long agricultural history of growing grapes, alfalfa, tomatoes, corn, beans and again grapes.

Initially Trentadue was undecided as to what types of grapes to plant. UC Davis suggested varietals, but old Italian wine families urged a mixed burgundy vineyard. As a compromise, the new owner selected mid-varietals such as Chenin Blanc and Gamay. In developing his winemaking skills, Trentadue absorbed the basics of the winemaking process from his father (who carves wine artifacts for the gift shop) and also gained much from friends in the wine business.

Originally the smaller ranch had a house, since enlarged, and two barns, one remodeled to be a makeshift winery and the other used for vineyard machinery. In 1973, construction commenced on a new winery building, which was designed with a tasting room and gift shop above and a wine cellar below.

The new winery building is surrounded by 144 acres of planted vineyard. Half the grapes are used at the winery; the other half are sold commercially.

Souverain Cellars

On a beautiful vine-laden knoll set against a backdrop of forest green stands the natural wood and native aggregate structure, Souverain Cellars. The building is virtually new, and the winemaking equipment inside as modern as tomorrow, yet the whole story of the original Souverain dates back to the early forties.

In 1943, Leland Stewart founded Souverain Cellars. He bought a 160-acre plot on Howell Mountain in the upper Napa Valley. It formerly belonged to Swiss immigrant Fulgenzio Rossini who ran a winery and vineyard until Prohibition. After Repeal, an attempt was made to revive the operation, but it soon fell into disuse for almost a decade.

As an innovative wine pioneer, Stewart learned all he could about fine winemaking. In 1949, he was the first individual to bottle and sell Green Hungarian as a varietal under its own name. Formerly, it had been used for blending generic wines. In that same year, he also released a Johannisberg Riesling and a Cabernet Sauvignon.

In 1970, Stewart sold Souverain Cellars to a group of investors and retired. Soon after, however, the Pillsbury Company acquired Souverain Cellars and established Souverain of Rutherford in the Napa Valley and Souverain of Alexander Valley in Sonoma County.

So it was that in 1972, John Marsh Davis, who had designed the Rutherford winery in a romantic image of a Napa Valley barn, was retained to build the new Sonoma winery. As his architectural theme, Davis selected the hop kiln which has now become a Sonoma trademark because of the one-time importance of the hop-growing industry and the unique architectural characteristics of the hop-drying barn. By 1973, the elegant winery and restaurant were completed. William Bonetti, formerly of Charles Krug and an alumnus of the School of Viticulture and Enology in Conegliano, Italy, was asked to be winemaker.

In the fall of 1973, Souverain crushed its first grapes. A policy was established to buy grapes from Sonoma County growers. The emphasis has been to select varieties from locales and micro-climates which have successfully developed a particular type of wine grape.

"We try to bring each vineyard of each variety to its optimum potential," states Bonetti. "There is no cookbook formula. We tailor our techniques to the variety, the vineyard and the traditional wine methods."

The winery is expensively equipped with American crusher-stemmers, French presses, stainless steel jacketed fermenters, a centrifuge, filters, stainless steel storage tanks and American and European oak tanks and barrels.

In 1976, the Pillsbury Company sold to North Coast Cellars, a partnership of North Coast grape growers. Souverain of Rutherford was sold to a group of partners, some of whom are associated with Freemark Abbey. The Souverain name, however, is retained by the Sonoma County facility for its premium wines.

A. Rafanelli Winery

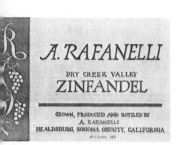

In Dry Creek Valley it is possible to find some of the original Italian homesteads first settled in Sonoma County. Mary and Americo Rafanelli live on a ranch which dates back nearly to the middle 1800's. Their farm is situated on West Dry Creek Road in Healdsburg.

In 1955, when the Rafanellis purchased a 100-acre working ranch, they had no intention of going into the winemaking business. They moved into a rambling white farmhouse with a spacious porch which encircles the house. The wooden barn and horse stables were used for storing ranch equipment.

In the beginning, the Rafanellis grew and sold pears and prunes. In the late sixties, when the demand for grapes began to increase, he replaced his orchards with vineyard.

Originally his grandfather had made wine at a winery near Florence. When Americo was a child, his father Albert Rafanelli, a contractor from San Francisco, bought a ranch in Healdsburg where the Healdsburg High School is now located. There the elderly Rafanelli had a vineyard and winery during the early 1940's.

Finally in 1974, homewinemaker Americo Rafanelli founded his winery. Once it was bonded, he began to restore the back barn built around the late 1800's with virgin redwood and square nails. Mary's father, Andrea Longo, a homewinemaker from San Francisco gave his old hand-operated basket press which Rafanelli uses to press grapes. The interior of the winery is equipped with redwood and oak cooperage. The winery is designed to produce 3,000 cases a year.

Presently Americo has 25 acres of vineyard. The vineyards are planted in gravelly loam and located in the hills and floor of Dry Creek Valley. The vineyard's varietals are Gamay Beaujolais, Zinfandel, Early Burgundy and French Colombard. The Dry Creek which gives the valley its name winds through the property just before joining the larger Russian River.

Americo Rafanelli takes pride in being responsible for every aspect of his operation. From sunrise to sunset he is in the vineyard or in the winery.

As he says, "I want to make only red wines. I want them to be big and full-flavored with a good amount of age. We plan to make pure wine with no chemicals and light or no filtering."

The winery makes three wines: Zinfandel, Gamay Beaujolais, and Early Burgundy. The wines' label will say "Dry Creek". In future years, the wines will be vintage-dated.

Nervo Winery

Frank Nervo, senior, arrived in the Sonoma Valley from Venice in 1896, with his 17-year-old bride, Maria. Drawn west by tales of wine flowing like water from the California valleys, Nervo bought 250 acres just north of Healdsburg, lying on two sides of the old Redwood Highway. The only cultivated land was ten acres of vineyard west of the highway on a knoll, where a small house was located. From the highway east to the Russian River was a tangle of oak trees and brush, which Nervo cleared, plowed and planted to grapes, principally Zinfandel, with some Alicante, Golden Chasselas, Malvasia and Carignane. In 1908 the present winery was constructed on a spur track of the railroad, from stone quarried in the hills above the Alexander Valley. Timbers for the roof and flooring were shipped from Oregon by rail, to the site. Redwood aging tanks were installed on the upper level and a small crusher place below. The must was piped upstairs by steam power and, after fermentation, was lowed by hand to the press. The finished wine was shipped in 50-gallon barrels by rail to New Orleans, Chicago, New York and San Francisco. Through the Prohibition years, the wine remained "sleeping" in the redwood tanks. When prohibition was repealed, the Nervos enlarged the winery and opened a retail sales room. Sales, at first, were Burgundy, Claret, Zinfandel and Sauterne, by the 50-gallon barrel. A new crusher with conveyor belt was set up with an overhead hoist to accommodate gondolas as well as box dumping. In 1955 the family pulled up much of the old vineyard and replaced it with varietal grapes: Pinot Noir, Pinot St. George, Beclan and Cabernet Sauvignon. As the grapes came of age, the Nervo Winery became a favorite stopping place and the reds, particularly the Nervo Zinfandel became famous. In 1970 the State started buying land to widen and re-route Highway 101. At first all the farmers from Lytton to Geyserville fought the freeway. Then, one by one, they sold to the State until only the Nervo Ranch was left. The new road wiped out the plantings of Beclan and a good portion of the famous Zinfandel.

In 1973, Julius Nervo approached the Jos. Schlitz Brewing Company, which had just purchased Geyser Peak Winery, and that fall the family sold the Nervo Winery and the 135 acres west of the highway to Geyser Peak.

The old redwood tanks were moved to the Frank Pastori Winery, north of Geyserville and the wine remained in storage until January 1976 when Julius opened a retail wine shop, The Wine Bank, in Geyserville. Still available, under the Pastori label and Julius Nervo's Geyserville Hills label, are Malvasia, a Beclan-Cabernet Sauvignon blend, Zinfandel, Chenin Blanc and Cabernet Sauvignon.

A line of nine wines, made and bottled by Nervo Winery, was introduced in 1975 and in the spring of 1976 five "country" wines were added. A pergola, shaded by vines, houses a picnic table and displays of restored antique equipment entrance visitors taking a brief respite from the high speed highway.

J. Pedroncelli Winery

Just over the Canyon Rd. foothills in the flat of the fog-shrouded Russian River watershed is the family-owned J. Pedroncelli Winery. At 16, John Pedroncelli came to California from the hills of Lombardy in Italy. Originally he homesteaded a 160-acre ranch near Pitt River. It is now covered by the Shasta Dam project. In 1927, he purchased the J. Canata Winery which was founded in 1904 by a wholesale grocer of that name.

On the property there was an old, red barn and a wood-frame house nestled against a hillside vineyard. A wine hobbyist, Pedroncelli began tinkering with the idea of growing and selling grapes to his friends, many of whom were also amateur winemakers. Eventually he cleared the land and planted a mixed burgundy vineyard. With hard work, he gradually built his avocation into a prosperous vocation. His line consisted of simple red and white wine and there were as yet no fancy varietals. Selling in barrel and gallon jugs, he counted on the patronage of the Italian colonies in and around San Francisco.

In 1963, James and John Pedroncelli took over the winery responsibilities from their father. Before long, they had increased their sales to 60,000 cases annually. At the same time, they improved the outer aesthetic appearance and the inner functional aspects of the winery. The wine cellar was painted a light tan and the winery exterior was resurfaced with redwood siding. The grounds were landscaped with red-berried manzanita, and an antique basket press and conservative but readily visible "winery" sign were placed by the roadside. Vaslin presses, stainless steel fermenters and storage tanks and small American and French oak barrels were acquired.

More than half their supply of grapes comes from their own 135-acre vineyard near the winery. Other grapes are purchased from growers in Dry Creek and Alexander Valley. The area is typified by its micro-climates and the presence of late summer fogs which follow the Russian River up the Pacific Ocean.

"The grapes from Dry Creek and Alexander Valley are chemically very similar," says John Pedroncelli, president. "Some varieties do better in some areas than others. Cabernet Sauvignon is good in Dry Creek. Johannisberg Riesling is good in the Alexander Valley. The weather does not present extremes and the gravelly loam puts out a more concentrated fruit."

Since the two brothers took over, their efforts have produced a marked improvement in the overall quality of Pedroncelli wines. Wisely, they have approached change cautiously. The extensive use of redwood so common of older Italian wineries has been minimized. The emphasis has turned to classical varietals with good varietal character. The Pinot Chardonnay and Cabernet Sauvignon are two good examples of wines which have benefited from the introduction of small oak and age.

The Pedroncelli Winery produces a limited line of other wines both white and red.

Geyser Peak Winery

The 3600 foot prominence of Geyser Peak names both the winery and the summit it faces. It was, in fact, the nearby geysers and mineral springs that lured German visitor Augustus Quitzow who constructed a handsome winery, north of Geyserville, in 1880. He soon added a sturdy distillery.

Quitzow sold in 1887 to a New York importer and wholesaler of quality brandies, Edward Walden. After the turn of the century the winery changed hands several times until 1937, when it was acquired by the Bagnani family, who retained the winery for 35 years.

Giuseppe Begnani made bulk wines at the Geyserville winery and his sons controlled the country's first vinegar company on Montgomery Street, in San Francisco. Known for their "Four Monks" label, the Bagnani family has been making wine vinegar since 1932 and continues to hold Federal Alcohol Tax Lic. No. 1.

When Giuseppe died in 1952, his son Dante took over the winery. He continued bulk wine production and says that he posted the following sign at the winery to discourage visitors: "Sorry, no retail sales. We drink it all."

The sleepy little winery began a rapid and sweeping transformation in 1972, when the Bagnani family voted to sell the operation to the Jos. Schlitz Brewing Company. Dante Bagnani was asked to stay on as vice-president of operations.

An old red barn was preserved to set the feeling and tempo for new winery construction. The grounds were landscaped with stone terraces, a flowing fountain, and wrought iron gates. The new winery, designed by noted winery architect Richard Keith, is composed of fieldstone and redwood, with a shake roof, and is molded gracefully into the adjacent hillside. The tasting room, also in redwood and stone, ties two eras of winemaking together. Inside, a series of stained-glass windows detail the story of grapes and wine. A new bottling facility and cooperage building are on the agenda.

Geyser Peak's aim is to produce "reasonable priced, premium quality California wines." To accomplish that goal, they recruited an experienced wine-maker, Al Huntsinger, who had been at Almaden for twenty years.

The first releases under Schlitz management bore "Voltaire" and "Summit" labels. The former are non-vintaged varietals and generics which are sold primarily to the restaurant trade. The latter is a jug line, with varietals like Cabernet Sauvignon and Napa Gamay joining the traditional trio of generics.

In 1976 the winery began releasing is premium line under the "Geyser Peak Winery" label. These are limited bottlings (less than 2500 cases each) of vintage-dated varietals, several of which are from specific appellations. Sonoma County Pinot Noir and Cabernet Sauvignon, from the 1974 vintage, highlight this line, which includes Chardonnay, Johannisberg Riesling, Chenin Blanc, a Rose' of Cabernet Sauvignon (the first of the line) and two generics.

Pastori Winery

It was only in 1974 that Frank Pastori started a winery and put the family name back in the wine business. His winery lies on the Old Redwood Highway on the southern boundary of Cloverdale, not too far from where it all began, and the tradition goes back a long way.

In the late 1800's the first Pastoris to come to California from northern Italy were Ermina and Constante. Hardy individuals, they settled in the desolate Signal Ridge area of Mendocino County. By 1910, they decided to move inland to a 110 acre ranch in the upper Russian River Valley in Somona County.

From the start, Constante's work reflected his independent nature. He grew his own grapes and made his own bulk wine. A major portion of the wine was sold to Italian Swiss Colony. The rest of the production was sold to other wineries. The original Pastori Winery operated in a bulk capacity until 1942. Then it was closed for several years after World War II when Giuseppe Mazzoni bought the property.

As a child Frank Pastori, son of the founder, had worked with his father at the winery. Later, he leased land from neighbor Frank Nervo and helped him run his uniquely designed stone winery.

Finally in the early seventies, Frank Pastori went into the wine business on his own when he built a winery on his Cloverdale ranch. The land extends from the Russian River to Dry Creek Ridge though it is divided by U.S. Highway 101. The view from the winery captures not only Geyser Peak, but Mt. St. Helena. In all, there are 50 acres of planted vineyards.

The present winery building, a converted prune hydrator, was developed in stages and eventually expanded as demand increased. Old redwood tanks stand side by side with newer stainless steel storage and oak cooperage. After Schlitz Brewing Company bought Nervo Winery, Frank Pastori acquired Nervo's 50,000 gallons of inventory. This stock became the foundation of his operation.

The Pastori tasting room is small and simple. Row after row of Pastori wines line the shelf. The label reveals that all the wines (which he now produces) are estate-bottled and vintage-dated with a "Northern Sonoma" designation of origin. The wines include Zinfandel, Pinot Noir, Pinot St. George, Johannisberg Riesling, Chenin Blanc, Sauterne, Burgundy and Vin Rose'.

Today the Pastori Winery generates between 10,000 and 12,000 cases annually. Frank Pastori believes in aging his red wines for approximately three to four years in wood. He uses large redwood vats, 50-gallon American white oak barrels and 60-gallon French Limousin oak casks. The white wines are made in stainless steel and held in a combination of stainless steel and oak cooperage. The varietals are available in fifths and the generics in gallons and half gallons.

After spending his life in the northern Sonoma countryside, Frank Pastori is convinced he resides in the "heart of the grape country."

Giuseppi Mazzoni

At the turn-of-the-century, Giuseppe Mazzoni left his home near the marble ruins in Carrara, Italy. When he arrived in California, he worked in the vegetable gardens in Colma south of San Francisco. By 1903, he had saved enough money to move to Sonoma County. There he purchased the 120-acre Butcher Ranch, which is located in Cloverdale. To Mazzoni, the area was reminiscent of Italy with its gently rolling hills and warm, sunny climate.

Originally the hillsides were blanketed with oak and madrone. After the land was cleared and prepared, two kinds of wine grapes were planted, Zinfandel and Carignane. On the tallest ridge on the property overlooking the lush countryside, Mazzoni erected a comfortable residence for his family and a sturdy wooden barn.

In 1912, Mazzoni divided his ranch into two farms; the upper ranchland, which runs into hilly back country and which was already developed, he gave to his next of kin; the lower ranchland, which runs into the valley, he selected as the site for his winery and kept for himself. At that time, Fred Mazzoni, present owner and vintner, along with his brother James, were mere youngsters and learned basic winemaking techniques from their father, Giuseppe.

When the winery was built, it was constructed of solid redwood timbers and outfitted with huge redwood tanks. Each year 80,000 gallons of bulk wine were sold to Italian Swiss Colony or the Petri Wine Co. The wine was taken in barrels by horse – drawn carriages to the old Chianti Depot (across from the Mazzoni Winery) then by rail to San Francisco.

During Prohibition, the winery went out of business, but in 1938, Fred Mazzoni reopened it again. Wines were bottled under the Mazzoni label and sold at Mazzoni's retail shop in San Francisco. Customers bought direct from the barrel until 1966 when the store was closed permanently.

In its heyday, the Mazzoni Winery was made up of a couple hundred acres of vineyard, which was later leased or sold. Today, Fred Mazzoni has only 40 acres of bearing vineyard, although he owns additional farmland. The Mazzoni family has historically been somewhat of a pioneer in promoting and producing high quality Zinfandel from the area. Because of the warm, northern Sonoma climate, their vines have produced exceptionally fruity berries with good sugar and natural acids.

Not wishing to work too hard in his advancing age, Mazzoni has reduced his production to around 4,000 cases a year. Three dry table wines are now available in gallons and half gallons: Zinfandel, Burgundy and Sauterne. Loyal customers who have been patronizing the winery for decades continue to stop in and visit.

"I learned winemaking from my father in the vineyard and in the cellar," explains 72-year-old Mazzoni. "I have always made heavy wine with lots of wood. I do not finish or pasteurize my wine."

Vina Vista Vineyards

Vina Vista Vineyard was so named in testimony to the panoramic view of Northern Sonoma County vineyard land that virtually surrounds the winery. Perched on a tall ridge in Geyserville, the winery also overlooks the northern Russian River region and Geyser Peak.

The winery and farm once belonged to Giuseppe Mazzoni and later passed to a married daughter. After her husband died, she and her children ran a successful bulk winery. In 1970, Keith Nelson, an engineer with Aeronuetronic Ford in Palo Alto, California, purchased the ranch and buildings.

In 1971, Nelson encouraged his engineering associates in Palo Alto to form a small corporation. Initially the group attempted to renovate the dilapidated barn and make it into a winery. Difficulties arose when they were prohibited by local building inspectors from using the building because of its run-down condition. Instead they constructed a new barn style redwood building. Over the front door, they placed a large hand-painted sign which says "Vina Vista Vineyards."

In addition to recycling some of the equipment which had been left behind, the new owners installed redwood tanks, stainless steel vats and small oak cooperage.

From the onset, the owners of Vina Vista Vineyards set up a program which would enable them to enter the wine business as soon as possible. Since the early seventies they have been buying bottled wine and champagne and marketing these products under the Vina Vista Vineyards label. The winery has six table wines and nine champagnes. Simultaneously, the owners began to make their own vintage-dated dry table wines. The wines made at the winery include Johannisberg Riesling, Zinfandel, Petite Sirah and Burgundy. The wines display a Sonoma appellation.

As plans progress, all the wine grapes will be purchased from reliable Sonoma growers At present the Vina Vista buys Zinfandel from Fred Mazzoni who lives nearby. A great believer in Zinfandel, Mazzoni has farmed the upper Sonoma wine region for several generations and finds the quality of grapes exceptional. Winemaker Nelson agrees. "I am rather intrigued with Zinfandel," he explains. "I want to make a couple of outstanding but definitely different styles of Zinfandel. I now have one Zinfandel which is heavy in body and another Zinfandel that is light in body. There is no better place to grow that grape than right here."

The owners of Vina Vista Vineyards feel that their wines should be young and fruity. For that reason they ferment their white wine in stainless steel. The red wines are handled in a more traditional manner with sufficient age in redwood and oak cooperage. Ultimately, the winery will strive to produce 14,000 cases and reduce their line to include four varietals.

A weekend visitor trying to find the winery could easily get lost on the way for there is no roadside sign. Vina Vista Vineyards is located on Chianti Road (the frontage road), west of U.S. Highway 101 driving north past Geyserville.

Italian Swiss Colony

Beside the rambling Russian River in the gently rolling vine-clad hills of northern Sonoma is Italian Swiss Colony.

The story of this historical Asti landmark goes back to the wisdoms and sympathies of its founder, Andrea Sbarboro. In 1850 at age 13, he came to San Francisco to assist his brother Batolomeo in the retail food and grocery business. At 25 the lad had amassed enough capital to open his own retail establishment. Then in 1873, the bank crisis in America changed his career and life. Sbarboro left the retail business and formed several mutual loan associations.

In 1881, business conditions still remained depressed. In San Francisco, there were many jobless and homeless Swiss and Italian emigrants who could hardly speak the new language. Sbarboro thought of forming a cooperative agricultural association where these people might work. He asked his closest friends for capital to be raised partly by installments paid by stockholders based on a building and loan association plan of one dollar a month per share for five years.

In March 1881, the Italian Swiss Agricultural Colony came into existence. On its board of Directors were many prominent members of the Italian community. They included Mark J. Fontana, president (and later chairman of a huge canning establishment); Dr. Giuseppe Ollino, vice president; Henry Cassanova, treasurer; Dr. Paola De Vecchi and Andrea Sbarboro, secretary. In 1881 Enrico Rossi, an enologist from the University of Turin joined the directors.

Searching throughout Sonoma County, Sbarboro discovered a picturesque setting similar to wine areas of northern Italy. The climate was warm, the soil was fertile and rainfall was abundant.

Raising $25,000 Sbarboro purchased 1500 acres of land smothered in oak and madrone. Once the land was cleared, Dr. Giuseppe Ollino, their vineyardist, selected and planted choice cuttings from Italy, France, Hungary and Germany. Their plan was merely to grow grapes.

But as the first grapes came to bear, the market price for them had dropped from $30 to $8 a ton. This unforseen situation led the directors to make a major decision to produce their own wine instead of try to sell the grapes and lose money. In 1887, additional funds were raised to construct a stone winery with 300,000 gallon capacity. That year, the wine turned to vinegar due to poor cellar treatment.

In spite of repeated misfortunes, loyal friends and backers stood behind the Colony. In 1888, the situation changed when enologist Enrico Rossi, an individual whose family had been grape growers and winemakers for generations in the Piedmont region of Italy, joined the firm. In a short time, he produced some remarkable dry table wines.

Again, when the directors tried to market their new product, they found they could get only seven cents a gallon in the market place. To remedy the situation, the association took on the role of agents and began to wholesale their own wine in New York, New Or-

El Carmelo Chapel at Asti

leans and Chicago. At last, Sbarboro could smile. The product was good and retailers paid anywhere from 30 to 50 cents a gallon. Eventually the Colony specialized in a Chianti, which was marketed in bottles enclosed in raffia, a wicker flask. The wine was called Tipo Chianti and quickly became very popular.

In 1901, in spite of the (Italian Swiss Agricultural Colony) original determination to remain independent of the CWA, the CWC affiliated with the CWA. The Colony became known as the Italian Swiss Colony (omitting agricultural). It was half owned by directors Sbarboro and Rossi and half owned by the powerful CWA.

In 1909 French champagnemaker Charles Jadeau was asked to come to Asti and experiment with sparkling wines which then were very much in demand. In spite of opposition from his countrymen, he came to taste and evaluate Sonoma white wines. Impressed with California and its wines, Rossi and Jadeau, with Rossi's half, raised capital for the champagne cellars. In 1911, their Golden Extra Dry Champagne won the highest prize, the Grand Prix, at the Exposition in Turin, Italy, The French were totally surprised.

In 1911, however, the talented Rossi was thrown from a horse and killed. After his tragic death, his two twin sons Edmund and Robert took over their father's responsibilities until the CWA bought out their half of the Colony. During Prohibition CWA liquidated its holdings and in 1920 the winery and vineyards were rebought by the Rossi twins and their friend Enrico Prati.

By 1894, the United States was in another depression. Many wineries pooled their grape resources and united under the California Wine Association (CWA). The owners of Italian Swiss Agricultural Colony, Sbarboro and Rossi, formed a rival syndicate (with which the winery was identified) called the California Wine Makers' Corporation (CWC). CWC believed that grape growers should have the option of selling their grapes to whomever they pleased with the right to bargain if necessary. The CWA was locked into grower-winery contracts at one set price.

During the early part of the twentieth century, Sbarboro remained as the secretary of the organization. During this time, he became very active in opposing the aims of the national Prohibition movement by delivering speeches, writing pamphlets and appearing before congressional committees. He believed that use of wines and temperance was the alternative to the use of hard liquor and Prohibiton. Gradually Sbarboro realized that he was only fighting a 'delaying action' and eventually resigned from the wine business, still a fighter at heart. In 1923 he died.

"In 1933," says Joe Vercelli, now manager of consumer relations for Italian Swiss Colony, "Asti was a community of first and second generation Italians. There were 20 homes, many along the creek beneath shade trees. There was a post office, railroad, church, one-room schoolhouse, a cookhouse, the Barella Bakery, a blacksmith with 25 teams of horses, vegetable gardens, goats, chickens and rabbits.

In 1942 National Distillers bought the operation from the Rossi twins and Enrico Prati. And in 1953 United Vintners, the present owners, purchased the vineyards and the winery.

Jade Mountain

JADE MOUNTAIN
Sonoma County
CABERNET SAUVIGNON
1973

Jade Mountain was founded in 1975 by Dr. Douglass Cartwright, a Jungian analyst, and his wife, Lillian Cartwright, a psychologist. Their charming wood and stone country house and their weathered wooden winery are located on their ranch in the rugged terrain southwest of Cloverdale.

The ranchland is made up of a series of hills and valleys, accented with canyons, glens and waterways. Doctor Cartwright named the dominant elevation which rises out of a chain of deeply wooded green mountains, Jade Mountain. The name Jade Mountain is the title of a Chinese anthology containing a collection of 300 poems from the T'ang Dynasty.

On the hillsides around the ranch are the remains of gnarled vineyards which Dr. Cartwright believes were planted by the early settlers in the late 1880's. In the late afternoon when the sun hits the hillsides at a certain angle, lines left from the furrowed vineyards may be seen. In the early 1900's the Newman family acquired the property which contained the remains of a working winery.

When Dr. Cartwright purchased the property in 1959, there were several old buildings badly in need of repair. In the barn, he found old pumps, wooden cooperage and wine artifacts which were used by the previous winemakers. In the early seventies, Dr. Cartwright renovated the old barn into a serviceable winery.

Surrounding the winery are 31 acres of vineyard located on the valley floor and hillsides. The additional pastureland is used to graze sheep and cattle while deer, quail and wild pig roam the back country. There are 19 acres of Cabernet Sauvignon; 7 acres of Riesling and five acres of hillside which have not been budded. Until 1974, the Cartwrights sold their grapes to other wineries. However, their enjoyment of fine wines led them to take a more serious approach to the art of winemaking.

The entire Cartwright family shares an interest in wines and rustic living. On weekends, it is not unusual to find the Cartwrights and their four children David, Derrick, Katy and Rosanna helping in the vineyard or winery. The children have found Pomo Indian arrowheads and pottery which were uncovered by tractors. A tall, lone pine dominates the hill above the vineyards. According to young Derrick Cartwright, an enthusiastic naturalist, it most likely is the burial site of a Pomo Indian chief.

As a 2,000 gallon producer, Jade Mountain will make only two vintage-dated, estate bottled selections, a German-style Riesling and a distinctive California Cabernet Sauvignon. Clarets are aged in 60 gallon French and Never oak casks.

"Our intent is to preserve a certain quality of family life in a positive, coperative farming venture at Jade Mountain. Life is less in the being and more in the becoming," concludes Dr. Douglass Cartwright.

Jade Mountain is an honest effort to create fine wine on a modest scale and budget with the enthusastic participation of family.

A. Rege Wine Co.

A. Rege Wine Co. is an example of how an older, small winery avoided getting caught up in the wine boom of the late sixties and early seventies. Instead, its owners chose to improve the quality of their vineyard and to combine good grapes with the tenets of winemaking passed down from their founder. Their formula has worked. Even their jug wines are well worth the asking, and there can be little criticism of their varietals considering the price.

Around 1900 Alfonso Rege came to San Francisco from northern Italy. For many years he worked in the sheet metal business, but in 1932, Alfonso ventured to Sonoma looking for land. Without much delay, he acquired the 52 acre Puchiro Ranch which had made something of a name for itself in the area as a producer of bulk wine.

Reges built a house and several farm buildings on top of a hill. On one side they could look at the Russian River and on the other side were the vineyards.

In 1939, without previous wine making experience, Alfonso made several batches of wine in the cellar below his house. Within time, he was able to build up a sizeable trade as people grew to respect the good quality of his bulk wine. As business increased, he opened a retail wine shop in San Francisco.

In 1947, brothers Eugene and Hector Rege, sons of founder Alfonso, took over the main responsibilities of the winery. And in 1963, they bought an adjoining ranch to increase their total holdings to 105 acres.

Today the family farms 78 acres of vineyard and purchases additional grapes from Sonoma growers. Since 1970, many of the older Rege vineyards, which contained as many as 15 different varieties, were replaced with Zinfandel.

"The climate in northern Sonoma is ideal for grapes. The days are in the nineties, hot and sunny; the nights are cooler," explains Eugene Rege, who heads the family business.

Annual wine production now averages 30,000 cases. The non-vintaged varietals available in fifths include Petite Sirah, Gamay Beaujolais and Cabernet Sauvignon. The Burgundy, Chablis, Sauterne and Rose' come in gallons. The winery features two labels, Chateau Rege and Alfonso Rege.

In 1937 when Alfonso Rege laid the concrete foundations for his sturdy redwood winery, he contemplated making wine simply. For the most part, the winery looks exactly as it did then, equipped with the traditional, large rewood tanks.

All the wines are fermented in large open concrete fermenters. Generally the bulk wines are aged for two years in redwood before they are released. The varietals are aged in small American white oak barrels and bottle.

A visit to the winery will find a friendly casual atmosphere at all times. Although there are no tours, the tasting room is opened on a daily basis.

To loyal customers, Rege jug wines mean "quality."

Bandiera Wines

Brillant red and green manzanita covers the faded white Bandiera Winery, located in the western foothills of Cloverdale. Across the rolling hills lie the Russian River and Pine Mountain.

In 1907, Emil Bandiera emigrated to California from Italy. He journeyed via Sonoma to the Mendocino Coast and settled in Greenwood, now called Elk. Employed as a lumberman, he helped fell some of the great coastal redwoods. In 1909, he and his wife, Liduina, moved to Cloverdale.

In 1927, the Bandieras purchased a 78 acre ranch adjacent to Cherry Creek Rd. They cleared the land and planted Zinfandel, Carignane, Grenoir and four acres of Golden Chasselas. Grapes were sold commercially, shipped by rail to Petaluma and then taken by boat to the open market on the San Francisco waterfront.

By 1935, a concrete and redwood winery was built. When the business opened in 1937 as Bandiera Wines, Inc., wine was sold by the barrel or hand-filled into casks and demi-johns at the winery. Wines were also bottled under the Bandiera label for retail trade. Today, the retail sales room reflects some of that old world flavor with its decorations of wicker flasks, wine bottles and historic labels.

As a youngster, Ralo D. Bandiera worked with his father in the winery, and following the senior Bandiera's death in 1964, became owner and wine-maker. In 1975, due to an unfortunate accident, Ralo was no longer able to make wine. Instead, he bought wine that was already made and bottled and sold it under his own label. Thus, winemaking ceased at Bandiera.

In July 1975, Chris Bilbro, grandson of Emil Bandiera, and Marc Black, descendant of an old Cloverdale family, bought the winery. Previously both men had worked at the winery.

As the 4,000 case winery is revitalized, new stainless steel fermenting tanks are put to use. Grapes will be acquired from three Sonoma sources: the 25-acre Bandiera Vineyards (now owned by Argonaut Constructors), the 60-acre Black Ranch and a plot on Sonoma Mountain.

The winery plans to make vintage-dated table wines which include Pinot Chardonnay, Cabernet Sauvignon, Petite Sirah, Pinot Noir, Zinfandel and one generic, Burgundy.

Once production gets going again, Bandiera Wines will feature two labels: Marca Bandiera (which means the flag brand in Italian) for the corked fifths and Bandiera for the cap-finished bulk wines. Gradually Bandiera will phase out buying bottled wines.

"We will make around 25 per cent varietals and 75 per cent jug wines. What we want to do is make a good, pure wine which is unfined and unfiltered," says winemaker Black.

The future of Bandiera Wines lies in the intelligent decisions and positive actions of its new, young owners, both enthusiastic to once again re-establish the Bandiera name in the competitive wine market.

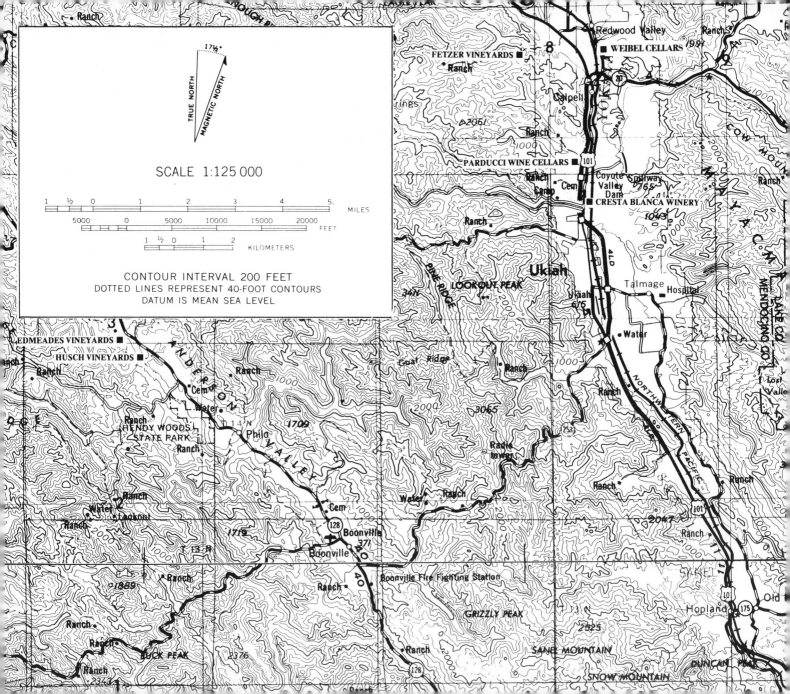

SCALE 1:125 000

MILES
1 ½ 0   1   2   3   4   5

5000   0   5000   10000   15000   20000   FEET

1 ½ 0   1   2   KILOMETERS

CONTOUR INTERVAL 200 FEET
DOTTED LINES REPRESENT 40-FOOT CONTOURS
DATUM IS MEAN SEA LEVEL

TRUE NORTH
MAGNETIC NORTH
17½°

FETZER VINEYARDS
WEIBEL CELLARS
Redwood Valley
Ranch
Ranch
Calpella
Ranch
△2061
PARDUCCI WINE CELLARS
101
Ranch
Cem
Coyote Valley Dam
Spillway 765
CRESTA BLANCA WINERY
1043
Ranch
LOOKOUT PEAK
PINE RIDGE
34N
Ukiah
Ukiah 575
Talmage
Hospital
Water

EDMEADES VINEYARDS
HUSCH VINEYARDS
Ranch
Ranch
Cem
Water
Ranch
HENDY WOODS
STATE PARK
Ranch
Philo
1709
Goat Ridge
Ranch
2000
3065
Radio Tower
253
Ranch
Ranch
Ranch
2047
Ranch
101

Ranch
Water
Lookout
Ranch
128
Boonville
371
Boonville
Cem
1719
13 A
Water
Ranch
Boonville Fire Fighting Station
GRIZZLY PEAK
SAND MOUNTAIN
Hopland
175
Old

Ranch
1889
Ranch
BUCK PEAK
2376
Ranch
Ranch
2425
SNOW MOUNTAIN
DUNCAN PEAK
128

Mendocino
Wineries

Cresta Blanca Winery

The original Cresta Blanca Winery was founded more than 90 years ago by Charles A. Wetmore. A reporter for the Newspaper *Alta California*, he was asked to do a comprehensive study of the state's wine industry. His investigations revealed that the inferior quality of wine in California was a reflection of the inferior quality of wine grapes. Not too much later, with the encouragement of the California State Viticultural Society, Wetmore attended the 1878 Paris Exposition and toured the vineyards of Europe where he had the opportunity to taste the wine and learn much more about its making.

During that period, Wetmore made the acquaintance of the Marquis de Lur Saluces, proprietor of Chateau d'Yquem. With his new friend's best wishes, Wetmore returned to the United States with cuttings from the four varieties which over the years had made the wines of Chateau d'Yquem famous. These were Semillion, Sauvignon Blanc, Colombard and Muscadelle de Bordelaise.

By 1883, Wetmore's vineyard in Alameda County near the town of Livermore was well established, and he began to make plans to construct a winery. Workmen excavated the limestone hills behind his property; the natural caves proved ideal for storing and aging wine. In 1889, the year of still another Paris Exposition, Wetmore returned to France where he entered his own wines in the competition. As one of some 17,000 wine entries, his Cresta Blanca wines placed first and received the highest prize, the Grand Prix.

In 1893, Clarence J. Wetmore, brother of Charles, purchased the winery, vineyards and name, Cresta Blanca. By 1895, the business became part of the larger Wetmore Bowen Co.; however, by 1913, the company was renamed the Cresta Blanca Wine Co. During Prohibition, Cresta Blanca produced sacramental and medicinal wines. In 1920, Lucien B. Johnson became owner. Fourteen years after Repeal, Johnson asked Clarence Wetmore to become president and then the original Wetmore Cresta Blanca relationship was reestablished.

In 1941, after Schenley Industries, Inc., purchased the Cresta Blanca Winery, the new organization announced its intention to reduce the line of table wines and to purchase grapes from vineyards all over California in addition to the winery's own 423 acres in the Livermore region.

In 1970, Cresta Blanca Winery was again sold, this time to Guild Wineries and Distilleries. The Cresta Blanca name was given to a former cooperative winery (one to which growers from the area sell their grapes to make bulk wine) located in Ukiah in Mendocino County. Today surrounding the winery there are 10 acres of vineyards. Aside from this production, the majority of the grapes are purchased from over 50 different growers within a 25 mile radius.

"In the future our emphasis will have a more direct tie with the Mendocino wine district," explains Gerald Furman, winery manager.

Parducci Wine Cellars

At the northern end of the Ukiah Valley, all but hidden in a small canyon beneath Pine Mountain Flat lies Parducci Winery.

Long ago, John Parducci and his wife came to the United States to share the wonders of California. They settled in the Santa Clara Valley and raised their four sons. In time, longing for their homeland took them back to Tuscany. This was in 1907, and young Adolph, later the winery founder, had just turned six. During his childhood, his father John taught him wine in the Italian vineyard and in the family winery.

Ten years later Adolph returned to the United States. Cloverdale, at the northern reaches of Sonoma County, became the site of his first American winery and vineyard. It was soon the home for his new Italian bride Isabella, and later birthplace of their four sons. Then misfortune struck and in the late 1920's the winery burned down and much of what Parducci had accomplished was destroyed. In search of a more permanent location, Parducci discovered Mendocino then an undeveloped but potentially productive wine district.

In 1932, Adolph Parducci commenced construction on his new facility at the 120-acre Pine Mountain Ranch. The property had once been used by the Pomo Indians for their pow-wows. Local gossip had it that the land had been the site of some of the first Mendocino vineyards.

In those early Mendocino days, Parducci Winery sold most of its wine production to a larger firm, Petri Wine Co. The rest went to special customers who brought their gallon jugs and demi-johns to the tasting room. It was jammed with rows of 50-gallon barrels which delivered wine from individual spigots. Wine was labeled and paid for at the door.

By 1976, four generations of Parducci had tried their skill at winemaking. In 1960, Adolph Parducci retired and left his four sons to carry on. In 1964, John and George Parducci bought out their younger brothers. In 1974, the two brothers formed a limited partnership with the Teachers Management Corp., Newport Beach, California. The Parduccis run the winery assisted by John's son, Richard, the fourth generation.

The hillside winery now has a new stone and redwood face. The inside glistens with stainless steel equipment, but some of the traditional redwood remains. The more recent buildings maintain a Spanish style. There is a bottling room and a storage area with a 700,000 capacity. The tasting room has a shake roof, stucco walls and stained glass windows. The grounds are landscaped with grapevines, olive trees and other cultivated foliage. The inside has tiled floors, beamed ceilings, wrought iron artwork and a fireplace.

Most of the grapes come from the 400 acres of vineyard on five nearby ranches, by name: Home, Talmage, Largo, Philo, and Kelseyville. Parducci has the distinction of being the first winery to plant Mendocino varietals.

Fetzer Vineyards

Fetzer
1974
ESTATE BOTTLED • MENDOCINO
CABERNET SAUVIGNON
PRODUCED AND BOTTLED BY
Fetzer Vineyards
REDWOOD VALLEY, CALIFORNIA
ALCOHOL 12% BY VOLUME

Redwood Valley is the home of Fetzer Vineyards in Mendocino County. Located 125 miles north of San Francisco, the 750-acre ranch runs along Forsythe and Seward Creeks at the headwaters of the Russian River.

For centuries, this region has been home for deer, bear, cougar, lion, bobcat, eagle, quail and blue heron. As one of the first ranches in Mendocino County, the Fetzer property was settled in 1849 by a successful gold miner, Anson Jebidiah Seward. With his gold, he was able to buy the ranch and build a colonial house and several out buildings. Seward planted grape cuttings and later constructed a winery.

In the middle 1950's, Bernard Fetzer, a manager for the Masonite Corp. bought the ranch from Jay Lee Smith. On the property there were 70 acres of vineyard, some of them dating back 100 years. Over a ten year period, the vineyards were replanted and enlarged. As an experiment, Fetzer planted Bordeaux-type varietals, including Cabernet Sauvignon, Semillon and Sauvignon Blanc. Air-freighting his grapes, he sold to home-winemakers in the United States and Canada. He found the market outside California to be a profitable alternative to the generally slackening local demand.

From 1964 to 1968, Fetzer leased four different vineyards for his business. The growing response from home winemakers convinced him of the worthiness of the Mendocino grape. The Cabernet Sauvignon was distinctively pleasing. In 1968, he started Fetzer Vineyards and produced 2,500 cases.

For a winery, he constructed timber and fieldstone buildings with mansard shake roofs and office tower. The 110 acres of vineyard sweep from ranch home on both sides of the two creeks through the Redwood Valley. Any additional grapes are purchased from other growers in Mendocino County and a small amount from Lake County.

Mendocino has made a name for itself due to its northerly position in relation to other wine areas in California. The cool nights contrasted by hot afternoons with minimal fog provide good growing conditions. The vines ripen almost two weeks later than in the Napa Valley.

Fetzer Vineyards has carved a niche for itself in the wine industry as a producer of quality red wine, which accounts for 80 per cent of the total production. The table wines include Cabernet Sauvignon, Petite Sirah, Zinfandel, Carmine Carignane, Fume' Blanc, Blanc de Blanc and Green Hungarian.

As winemaker, John Fetzer stresses heavy red wines and young white wines. The whites are held in different sizes of Yugoslavian oak. The reds are aged in the 2,000-barrel cellars. Production is 50,000 cases a year.

"The great and exciting things about wine are the soil, the climate, the vinification and the blending. I used to think you had to be a purist (and make 100 per cent varietals). To me, one of the most exciting aspects is the blending."

Husch Vineyards

HUSCH VINEYARDS
MENDOCINO
Pinot Chardonnay
Estate 1975 Bottled

Grown, Produced and Bottled by Husch Vineyards
Philo, California
ALCOHOL 13.7% BY VOLUME

Tony and Gretchen Husch had not ordered their lives in preparation for the profession of winegrower. Their common meeting ground, in fact, had been graduate work in city planning at the University of California at Berkeley. Tony, a native of St. Louis, Missouri, had done his undergraduate work at Harvard. Gretchen, who grew up in Maryland and is a Sarah Lawrence alum, is an artist.

The young couple resolved to quit the city for the less complex country life when Tony expressed a strong desire "to plant grapes and make wine." So they bought sixty acres of the Nunn Ranch, known formerly for its apple and grain production. In 1968 they planted their first eight acres of vines on slopes with southern exposure, which sweep down towards the Navarro River. They now have nearly twenty-five terraced, trellised acres in three varieties: Pinot Noir, Chardonnay, and Gewurztraminer. All are admirably suited to the cool Anderson Valley clime. The Pacific Ocean is but twelve air miles west and early morning fogs often keep thermometer readings noticeably lower than in the Ukiah or Redwood Valley areas. Grapes mature slowly, retaining acidity; the wines thus retain a good deal of their varietal character.

In 1971 a small outbuilding was bonded and wine-making began. Grapes, picked by hand into forty-pound lug boxes, were crushed on the patio of the Husch home, framed by the vineyards behind. As the couple gained experience their operation slowly grew. Chemist Al White, who had met Tony while buying a house from him, joined the Husches in 1973. The following year a new and well-equipped winery, whose exterior was designed to look like the barns common to the region, was built. Its 10,000 gallon capacity will handle the full production of the vineyards, which suits the Husches just fine. It has always been their policy to produce wines only from their own fruit.

Only four wines are produced at Husch Vineyards. All, save the rose', are made solely from the variety named. The Husch Pinot Noir Rose' is a blend of Pinot Noir and Chardonnay.

The Husch winery is located at the western end of the Anderson Valley, about midway between Philo and Navarro on California State Highway 128. Next to the winery is the sales and tasting room, aesthetically remodeled from an old granary. In addition to the Husch wines, Gretchen's watercolors of vineyards, other landscapes, and seascapes are also on display and for sale. The tasting room is open daily from ten to five and visitors are invited to make use of a shady picnic area, with deck, view, and tables.

The winery's label, which Gretchen designed, shows a young couple silhouetted in a row of vines. It is an expression of the idealism and vitality brought to their new vocation by Gretchen and Tony Husch.

Edmeades Vineyards

Tall and elegant, a California cypress spreads its branches out over Edmeades Vineyards in southwestern Mendocino County. Established in 1962 by Dr. Donald Edmeades, formerly of Pasadena, California, this picturesque winery rests on a hill above Anderson Valley.

As he approached retirement, Dr. Edmeades developed enthusiasm for winemaking and a good place to raise grapes. He discovered and purchased a 100 acre apple ranch in Philo, not far from the California coast.

As the demand for wine increased in the late sixties, Dr. Edmeades started with 10 acres of nursery stock. On the recommendation of UC Davis viticultural experts, Dr. Edmeades planted Chardonnay, Gewurztraminer, French Colombard and Cabernet Sauvignon. He was very successful and found the quality of grapes produced to be excellent. Originally, he sold his grapes commercially to the Parducci Winery in Ukiah.

After Dr. Edmeades died in 1972, his son Deron and Deron's wife, Pam, took over the property. Together they decided to make their own wine and continue to sell some of their grapes as well.

The apple dryer below the main house was converted into a two-story winery. It was paneled and insulated, and by 1975, it was fully equipped with modern stainless steel, jacketed fermenters. A range of wooden cooperage was bought, which included 135-gallon French oak ovals, small 50-gallon American oak casks and Yugoslavian uprights. Directly adjacent to the winery lies the new redwood case storage building. Next to the ranch house is the tasting room, a rustic but practical structure made from an old, lean-to-type shed.

Edmeades Vineyards now has 65 acres of vineyard located on land above the Navarro River. The vineyards are made up of Chardonnay, Gewurztraminer, French Colombard and Cabernet Sauvignon. Edmeades purchases its Zinfandel and any other wine grapes it might need from local Anderson Valley growers.

After experimenting with a wide assortment of table wines, the owners of this 2,000-case winery have narrowed their list to include the following wines: Chardonnay, Johannisberg Riesling, Gewurztraminer, Cabernet Sauvignon, Pinot Noir and Zinfandel. All the premium varietals are vintage-dated and show their Mendocino origin on the label. The winery also makes two generics—a Mendocino Red and a Mendocino White. The newest item, Apple wine, displays the Anderson Valley designation on the label.

"We are trying to make a quality product," says Deron Edmeades, owner. "We want to emphasize the Anderson Valley as the most northern wine region in Mendocino County. It has a cool climate and a long growing season. It is excellent for such varieties as Chardonnay, Gewurztraminer and Pinot Noir."

In 1976, Edmeades Vineyards opened a tasting room on Main St. of the coastal town of Mendocino. This is in addition to their tasting room at the winery which is opened for visitors on a daily basis.

Other Wineries

Bill Baird, owner of BALVERNE CELLARS, has planted 250 acres of grapes on 710 acres of rolling hills outside Windsor with first wines scheduled for release in 1978. Construction of a winery building will be complete in 1979.

The BELIZ-DE LOACH winemaking operation released their first wine in 1977, a 1975 vintaged Zinfandel. Until a winemaking facility is constructed, warehouse space is being leased in Santa Rosa. Bottling will also be done under the Willowside Vineyards label.

In 1971, Sandy and John Dach left their home on the outskirts of San Jose where they had a small, do-it-self winery called Bear Creek Vineyards. Relocating in the Anderson Valley in Mendocino County, they founded DACH VINEYARDS. They have planted 20 acres of such varieties as Chardonnay, Gewurztraminer and Pinot Noir. In 1976, the 1000 to 1500 case Dach Vineyards will make its first wines (from grapes which they will buy) in their new winery building.

DEHLINGER WINERY is being built by the Dehlinger family Tom, Klaus and Dan. Their 14 acre vineyard surrounds the redwood winery and is planted to Chardonnay, Pinot Noir and Cabernet Sauvignon. Their rolling hillside vineyards are in Forestville midway between Santa Rosa and Sebastopol.

The original CHRIS A. FREDSON WINERY was founded in 1890 by Israel Fredson from Sweden. Located between Healdsburg and Geyserville, it was yet another of the important bulk wineries which formed the backbone of Sonoma's early wine history. In the 1950's when U.S. Highway 101 was aligned through northern Sonoma County, the property on which the winery was located was in the path of progress and sold to the state as a right of way. Owners Donald and Leonard Fredson, sons of the founder, bought another winery, the old Dry Creek Vineyards, and then resumed business in the picturesque Dry Creek Valley. Business continues operations today with an assist by Donald's son, Robert. Wine is made and sold to Charles Krug Winery of the Napa Valley.

The FREI BROS. WINERY was founded in 1880 by a German immigrant Jay Fost, as a small 4,000 gallon winery. It is located on Dry Creek Rd. in Healdsburg. In 1883, the winery was bought and run by Swiss-German Andrew Frei, who in 1905 turned the business over to his two sons Walter and Louis. Today, it is one of the largest bulk wineries in Sonoma County and Andrew Frei, great grandson of the original Andrew, shares an active partnership with Ernest & Julio Gallo of the Gallo Winery in Modesto, California.

JORDAN VINEYARDS is one of the most elaborate new winery ventures to establish in the Alexander Valley in the last decade. Conceived on a grand but tasteful scale, the proposed winery and country inn were just getting underway in mid-1976. The winery is owned by Tom Jordan of Colorado and is scheduled for completion in 1981 when the 1976 Cabernet Sauvignon will probably be released.

LAMBERT BRIDGE WINERY is another sophisticated and costly new winery being built in the Dry Creek Valley. Owned by C. L. Lambert of San Francisco, the proposed 12,000 case winery will be located on property which was formerly used as a technical school in the 1860's on W. Dry Creek Rd. According to winemaker Edward Samperton, the first premium table wines will not be available until 1980.

The NAVARRO WINERY in Philo is named after the rambling Navarro River which runs through the Anderson Valley in Mendocino County. Founded in the early seventies by Edward T. Bennett of San Francisco, the less-than-a-1000 case winery has the distinction of being one of the first wineries in the Anderson Valley to build its winery first before planting its grapes. The owner has planted 15 acres of Cabernet Sauvignon, Gewurztraminer and Pinot Noir. The wines will be released in the late seventies.

Further up W. Dry Creek Rd. is another new wine enterprise, PRESTON WINERY. Louis D. Preston comes from a long-time north county farming family. His folks had a dairy, orchards, and vineyards near Windsor and Louis, after an Army stint and an MBA from Stanford, managed their ranch. A year at U.C. Davis turned Louis toward winegrowing. He bought a small ranch in Healdsburg and converted a 1917 prune dehydrator into a 2000 case winery in 1975.

The fourth generation SEGHESIO WINERY, INC., is one of the oldest bulk wineries still in operation in northern Sonoma County. Founded in 1902 by Edward Seghesio from Asti, Italy, the business was operated for many years by his two sons Arthur and Eugene. Although today Arthur is retired, Eugene and Arthur's son Edward manage two substantial operations in Healdsburg and Cloverdale. Presently, Seghesio Winery, Inc., sells a major part of its wine to Paul Masson and Gallo. In 1978, the winery owners will also bottle wine under their own label.

SONOMA COUNTY CELLARS was founded near the turn-of-the-century by Frank and Rachele Passalacqua, some of the earliest settlers in the Healdsburg area. The winery was given to son Emil Passalacqua, and then later acquired by his sister, the present owner, Edith Passalacqua. Today the winery is used solely as an aging cellar for Paul Masson.

The SONOMA COUNTY COOPERATIVE in Windsor is one of the original wineries established by the distinguished wine firm of Kohler & Frohling. During the height of its production, Kohler & Frohling owned wineries throughout the major wine districts of California. In the early thirties, the cooperative was organized for area growers. Since then, it was bought by E & J Gallo Winery and remains under their direction.

WEIBEL CHAMPAGNE VINEYARDS was originally established at the historic Mission San Jose in Alameda County where the main winery facilities remain to this day. Beginning in 1965 founder Fred Weibel purchased 480 acres of land in the Redwood Valley outside of Ukiah near the headwaters of the Russian River. Weibel now maintains a visitor's center in Ukiah, a brick structure whimsically designed to resemble an upturned champagne glass.

Appendix

ALEXANDER VALLEY VINEYARDS   Page 133
Address: 8644 Highway 128, Healdsburg, Calif., 95448
Phone: (707) 433-6293
Hours: 10-5 daily
Facilities: Tours by apppointment, tasting, sales
Winemaker: Harry (Hank) Wetzel, III
Wines: varietal
Vineyards: 250 acres
Volume: 18,000 gallons fermenting, 18,000 gallons storage, 7,000 cases annually

BANDIERA WINES   Page 169
Address: 155 Cherry Creek Rd., Cloverdale, Calif. 95476
Phone: (707) 894-2352
Hours: 1-5 daily
Facilities: sales
Winemaker: Marc H. Black
Vineyards: winery buys all grapes
Volume: 10,000 gallons fermenting, 75,000 gallons storage, 4,000 cases annually

BUENA VISTA WINERY   Page 87
Address: 18000 Old Winery Rd., Sonoma, Calif., 95476
Phone: (707) 938-8504
Hours: 9:30-5 daily
Facilities: self-guided tour, tasting and sales
Winemaker: Rene G. Lacasia
Wines: varietal, generic, dessert and champagne
Vineyards: 750 acres
Volume: 5,977 gallons fermenting, 190,046 gallons storage, 30,000 cases annually, 200,000 as winery expands.

CAMBIASO WINERY & VINEYARDS   Page 129
Address: 1141 Grant Ave., Healdsburg, Calif., 95448
Phone: (707) 433-5508
Hours: By special sppointment
Facilities: retail sales 10-3 daily except Wed. & Thurs.
Winemaker: Joseph Cambiaso
Wines: varietal and generic
Vineyards: 35 acres
Volume: 250,000 gallons fermenting, 750,000 gallons storage, 80,000 cases annually

CHATEAU ST. JEAN   Page 99
Address: 8555 Sonoma Highway, Kenwood, Calif., 95452
Phone: (707) 833-4134
Hours: 10-4:30 daily
Facilities: tours by appointment, tasting, sales
Winemaker: Richard Arrowood
Wines: varietals and champagne
Vineyards: 100 acres
Volume: 69,000 gallons fermenting, 130,000 gallons storage, 30,000 cases annually

CRESTA BLANCA WINERY   Page 173
Address: 2399 North State St., Ukiah, Calif., 95482
Phone: (707) 462-5161, (415) 956-6330
Hours: 9-5 daily
Facilities: tours by request, tasting, sales
Winemaker: Gerald Furman
Wines: varietal, generic, champagne, dessert
Vineyards: 10 acres
Volume: 500,000 gallons fermenting, 1,000,000 gallons storage,

DAVIS BYNUM WINERY   Page 115
Address: 8075 Westside Rd., Healdsburg, Calif., 95448
Phone: (707) 433-5852
Hours: tours by special appointment
Facilities: sales only
Winemaker: Davis Bynum
Wines: varietal
Vineyards: purchased grapes
Volume: 80,000 gallons fermenting, 80,000 gallons storage, 15,000 cases annually

DRY CREEK VINEYARD   Page 141
Address: 3770 Lambert Bridge Rd., Healdsburg, Calif., 95448
Phone: (707) 433-1000
Hours: 10-5 daily in summer
Facilities: tours, tasting, sales
Winemaker: David S. Stare
Wines: varietal and generic
Vineyards: 50 acres
Volume: 25,000 gallons fermenting, 60,000 gallons storage, 12,000 cases annually

EDMEADES VINEYARDS   Page 181
Address: 5500 California Ste. Hwy. 128, Philo, Calif., 95466
Phone: (707) 895-3232
Hours: 11-6 daily
Facilities: tours, tasting, sales
Winemaker: Jed Steele
Wines: varietal and generic
Vineyards: 35 acres
Volume: 15,000 gallons fermenting, 21,000 gallons storage, 9,000 cases annually

FETZER VINEYARDS   Page 177
Address: 1150 Bel Arbes Rd., Redwood Valley, Valif., 95470
Phone: (707) 485-8998
Hours: By special appt. call (707) 485-8802
Facilities: tours by appointment; tasting and sales 9:30-5 in Hopland
Winemaker: John Fetzer
Wines: varietal and generic
Vineyards: 120 acres
Volume: 200,000 gallons fermenting, 300,000 gallons storage, 55,000 cases annually

FOPPIANO VINEYARDS   Page 125
Address: 12707 Old Redwood Hwy., Healdsburg, Calif., 95448
Phone (707) 433-1937
Hours: 10-4:30 daily
Facilities: tours by appointment, tasting and sales
Winemaker: August Foppiano
Wines: varietal and generic
Vineyards: 200 acres
Volume: 100,000 gallons fermenting, 1,000,000 gallons storage, 150,000 cases annually

GEYSER PEAK WINERY   Page 153
Address: 3775 Thornsberry Rd., Geyserville, Calif., 95441
Phone: (707) 433-5349
Hours: 10-5 weekends, or by special appointment
Facilities: tours by appointment, retail sales, no tasting
Winemaker: Al Huntsinger
Wines: varietal and generic
Vineyards: 325 acres
Volume: 600,000 gallons fermenting, 30,000 gallons storage, 3,000 cases annually now, eventually 20,000

GRAND CRU VINEYARDS   Page 97
Address: 1 Vintage Lane, Glen Ellen, Calif., 95442
Phone: (707) 996-8100
Hours: 10-5 Sat. & Sun. only
Facilities: informal tours, tasting, sales
Winemaker: Robert L. Magnani
Wines: varietal
Vineyards: 36 acres
Volume: 40,000 gallons fermenting, 50,000 gallons storage, 10,000 cases annually, 20,000 eventually

GUNDLACH BUNDSCHU WINE CO.   Page 79
Address: 3773 Thornsberry Rd., Vineburg, Calif., 95487
Phone: (707) 938-5277
Hours: Noon-5 Fri., Sat., & Sun.
Facilities: informal tours, rasting, retail sales
Winemaker: John Merritt
Wines: varietal
Vineyards: 300 acres
Volume: 10,000 gallons fermenting, 15,000 gallons storage, 3,500 cases annually

HACIENDA WINE CELLARS   Page 91
Address: 1000 Vineyard Lane, Sonoma, Calif., 95476
Phone: (707) 938-3229, 938-2244
Hours: 10-5:30 daily
Facilities: yours by appointment only, tasting, sales
Winemaker: Steve MacRostie
Wines: varietal and dessert
Vineyards: 60 acres
Volume: 5,000 gallons fermenting, 20,000 gallons storage, 4,000 cases annually

HANZELL VINEYARDS   Page 93
Address: 18596 Lomita Ave., Sonoma, Calif., 95476
Phone: (707) 996-3860
Hours: 8-5 daily
Facilities: tours, sales, no tasting
Winemaker: Robert Sessions
Wines: varietal
Vineyards: 29 acres
Volume: 5,600 gallons fermenting, 11,000 gallons storage, 2,400-3,500 cases annually

HOP KILN WINERY   Page 117
Address: 6050 Westside Rd., Healdsburg, Calif., 95448
Phone: (707) 433-6491
Hours: Tours by special appointment
Facilities: tours, tasting, sales
Wines: varietal
Winemaker: Dr. L. Martin Griffin, Jr.
Vineyards: 65 acres
Volume: 6,000 gallons fermenting, 9,000 gallons storage, 3,000-4,500 cases annually

HUSCH VINEYARDS   Page 179
Address: 4900 Calif. Ste. Hwy. 128, Philo, Calif., 95446
Phone: (707) 895-3216
Hours: 9-5 daily
Facilities: tours, tasting, sales
Winemaker: Wilton (Tony) Husch
Wines: varietal
Vineyards: 20 acres
Volume: 2,000 gallons fermenting, 5,000 gallons storage, 1,500 cases annually

ITALIAN SWISS COLONY   Page 161
Address: Asti, Calif.
Phone: (707) 894-2541
Hours: 10-5 daily
Facilities: tours, tasting, sales
Winemaker: Robert B. Rife'
Wines: varietals, generics, dessert
Vineyards: 600 acres

JADE MOUNTAIN   Page 165
Address: 1335 Hiatt Rd., Cloverdale, Calif., 95425
Phone: please write letter
Hours: not open to public
Facilities: no tours or tasting
Winemaker: Dr. Douglas Cartwright
Wines: varietal
Vineyards: 35 acres
Volume: 2,000 gallons fermenting, 5,000 gallons storage,
2,000 cases annually

JOHNSONS' OF ALEXANDER VALLEY   Page 135
Address: 8333 Calif. Ste. Hwy. 128, Healdsburg, Calif. 95448
Phone: (707) 433-2319
Hours: 10-5 daily
Facilities: tours, tasting, sales
Winemaker: Tom Johnson
Wines: varietal and fruit
Vineyards: 40 acres
Volume: 5,000 gallons fermenting, 150,000 gallons storage,
3,000 cases annually, 12,000 eventualy

KENWOOD VINEYARDS   Page 101
Address: 9592 Sonoma Highway, Kenwood, Calif., 95452
Phone: (707) 833-5891
Hours: 9-5 daily
Facilities: tours by appointment only, tasting, sales
Winemaker: Robert Kozlowski and Michael Lee
Wines: varietal
Vineyards: 20 acres, lease 100 additional acres
Volume: 60,000 gallons fermenting, 200,000 gallons storage,
20,000 cases annually

KORBEL & BROS., F.   Page 111
Address: Guerneville, Calif., 95446
Phone: (707) 887-2294
Hours: 9:45-5:30 daily
Facilities: tours, tasting, sales
Winemaker: Adolph Heck champagne master; Allan Hemphill
and Jim Huntsinger, winemakers
Wines: varietal, generic, champagne and brandy
Vineyards: 600 acres
Volume: 100,000 gallons fermenting, 1,000,000 gallons storage,
200,000 cases champagne, 500,000 cases brandy, 100,000 cases
wine annually

LANDMARK VINEYARDS   Page 121
Address: 9150 Los Amigos Rd., Windsor, Calif., 95492
Phone: (707) 838-9466
Hours: by special appointment
Facilities: tours, tasting, sales
Winemaker: William Mabry III
Wines: varietal
Vineyards: 90 acres
Volume: 10,000 gallons fermenting, 12,000 gallons storage,
3,000-4,000 cases annually

MARTINI & PRATI WINES, INC.   Page 107
Address: 2191 Laguna Rd., Santa Rosa, Calif., 95401
Phone: (707) 823-2404
Hours: 9-4 Mon.-Fri.
Facilities: tasting, sales, no tours
Winemaker: Frank Vanucci
Wines: varietal, generic and dessert
Vineyards: 62 acres
Volume: 270,000 gallons fermenting, 2,000,000 gallons storage,
500,000 gallons annually with 20,000 devoted to cases

MAZZONI WINERY   Page 157
Address: 23645 Redwood Highway, Cloverdale, Calif., 95427
Phone: (707) 857-3691
Hours: 9-5
Facilities: retail sales, no tours or tasting
Winemaker: Fred Mazzoni
Wines: varietal and generic
Volume: 30,000 gallons fermenting, 110,000 gallons storage,
4,000 cases annually

MILL CREEK VINEYARDS   Page 119
Address: 1401 Westside Rd., Healdsburg, Calif., 95448
Phone: (707) 433-5098
Hours: 10-5 weekends
Facilities: no tours or retail sales
Winemaker: James Kreck; Robert Stemmler-Consultant
Wines: varietal
Vineyards: 75 acres
Volume: 20,000 gallons fermenting, 46,000 gallons storage,
4,500 cases annually now, 10,000 later

NERVO WINERY   Page 149
Address: Independence Lane exit, east from Hwy 101, Geyser-
ville, Calif., 95411
Phone: (707) 857-3417
Hours: 10-5 daily
Facilities: tasting, picnic tables
Winemaker: Al Huntsinger
Wines: varietal, generic, dessert
Vineyards: 137 acres
Volume: 200,000 gallons storage, all bulk sales-no cases

PARDUCCI WINE CELLARS __Page 175
    Address: 501 Parducci Rd., Ukiah, Calif., 95482
    Phone: (707) 462-3828
    Hours: 9-5 winter, 8-6 summer daily
    Facilities: tours, tasting, sales
    Winemaker: John A. Parducci
    Wines: varietal and generic
    Vineyards: 230 acres
    Volume: 2,000,000 gallons fermenting, 1,125,000 gallons storage, 175,000 cases annually

PASTORI WINERY __Page 155
    Address: 23189 Redwood Highway, Cloverdale, Calif., 95425
    Phone: (707) 857-3418
    Hours: 9-5 daily
    Facilities: tours, tasting, sales
    Winemaker: Frank Pastori
    Wines: varietal and generic
    Vineyards: 50 acres
    Volume: 65,000 gallons storage, 10,000-12,000 cases annually

PEDRONCELLI WINERY, J. __Page 151
    Address: 1220 Canyon Rd., Geyserville, Calif. 95441
    Phone: (707) 857-3619
    Hours: 10-5 daily
    Facilities: tasting, sales, no tours
    Winemaker: John Pedroncelli
    Wines: varietal and generic
    Vineyards: 135 acres
    Volume: 140,000 gallons fermenting, 520,000 gallons storage, 90,000 cases

RAFANELLI WINERY __Page 147
    Address: 4685 West Dry Creek Rd., Healdsburg, CAlif., 95448
    Phone: (707) 433-1385
    Hours: by special appointment or telephone call
    Facilities: Retail sales, no tours or tasting
    Winemaker: Americo Rafanelli
    Wines: varietal and generic
    Vineyards: 25 acres
    Volume: 10,000 gallons storage, 2,000 cases annually

REGE WINE CO. __Page 167
    Address: 26700 Dutcher Creek Rd., Cloverdale, Ca., 95425
    Phone: (707) 894-2953
    Hours: 9-5 daily
    Facilities: no tours, tasting and sales
    Winemaker: Eugene Rege
    Wines: varietal and generic
    Vineyards: 78 acres
    Volume: 150,000 gallons storage, 30,000 cases annually

RUSSIAN RIVER VINEYARDS __Page 109
    Address: 5700 Gravenstein Hwy., Forestville, Calif., 95436
    Phone: (707) 887-2243
    Hours: by special appointment
    Facilities: tours, tasting, sales
    Winemaker: Robert Lasden
    Wines: varietal and generic
    Vineyards: 27 acres
    Volume: 2,000 gallons fermenting, 10,000 gallons storage, 5,000 cases annually

SAUSAL WINERY __Page 137
    Address: 7370 Calif. Ste. Hwy. 128, Healdsburg, Calif., 95448
    Phone: (707) 433-2285
    Hours: by special appointment
    Facilities: tasting, retail sales, no tours
    Winemaker: David Demostene
    Wines: varietal and generic
    Vineyards: 150 acres
    Volume: 125,000 gallons storage, 50,000 cases annually

SEBASTIANI VINEYARDS __Page 83
    Address: 389 Fourth St. E., Sonoma, Calif., 94576
    Phone: (707) 938-5532
    Hours: 10-5 daily
    Facilities: tours, tasting, sales
    Winemaker: August Sebastiani
    Wines: varietal, generic, dessert
    Vineyards: 400 acres
    Volume: 500,000 gallons fermenting, 5,000,000 gallons storage, 1,500,000 cases annually

SIMI WINERY __Page 139
    Address: 16275 Healdsburg Ave., Healdsburg, Calif., 95448
    Phone: (707) 433-6981
    Hours: 10-5 daily
    Facilities: tours, tasting, sales
    Winemaker: Mary Ann Graf
    Wines: varietal
    Volume: 275,000 gallons fermenting, 583,000 gallons storage, 90,000 cases annually

SONOMA VINEYARDS __Page 123
    Address: 11455 Old Redwood Highway, Windsor, Calif., 95492
    Phone: (707) 433-6511
    Hours: 10-5 daily
    Facilities: tours by appointment only; tasting, sales
    Winemaker: Rodney D. Strong
    Wines: varietal and generic
    Vineyards: 650 acres
    Volume: 1,000,000 gallons fermenting, 3,500,000 gallons storage, 250,000 cases annually

SOTOYOME WINERY   Page 127
  Address: 641 Limerick Lane, Healdsburg, Calif., 95448
  Phone: (707) 433-2001
  Hours: by appointment
  Facilities: tours, tasting, sales
  Winemaker: John C. Stampfl
  Wines: varietal
  Vineyards: 15 acres
  Volume: 8,000 gallons fermenting, 30,000 gallons storage, 4,000 cases annually

SOUVERAIN CELLARS   Page 145
  Address: 400 Souverain Rd., Geyserville, Calif., 95411
  Phone: (707) 433-6918
  Hours: 10-5 daily
  Facilities: tours, tasting, sales
  Winemaker: William Bonetti and Dave Henry
  Wines: varietal and generic
  Vineyards: 3 acres
  Volume: 600,000 gallons fermenting, 2,500,000 gallons storage, 200,000 cases annually

JOSEPH SWAN VINEYARDS   Page 105
  Address: 2916 Laguna Rd., Forestville, Calif., 95436
  Phone: (707) 546-7711
  Hours: not open to the public
  Facilities: none
  Winemaker: Joseph Swan
  Wines: varietal
  Vineyards: 10½ acres
  Volume: 3,000 gallons fermenting, 2,400 gallons storage, 1,500 cases annually

TRENTADUE WINERY   Page 143
  Address: 19170 Old Redwood Hwy., Geyserville, Calif., 95441
  Phone: (707) 433-3104
  Hours: 10-5 daily
  Facilities: tasting, sales, gift shop
  Winemaker: Leo Trentadue
  Wines: varietal
  Vineyards: 200 acres
  Volume: 22,000 gallons fermenting, 100,000 gallons storage, 12,000 cases annually

VALLEY OF THE MOON WINERY   Page 95
  Address: 777 Madrone Rd., Glen Ellen, Calif., 95442
  Phone: (707) 996-6941
  Hours: 9-5 daily except Thursday
  Facilities: Tasting, sales, no tours
  Winemaker: Harry Parducci & Otto Toschi
  Wines: varietal, generic, dessert
  Vineyards: 200 acres
  Volume: 40,000 gallons fermenting, 200,000 gallons storage, 83,000 cases annually

VINA VISTA VINEYARDS   Page 159
  Address: Chianti Rd., Geyserville, Calif., 95441
  Phone: (415) 967-1824
  Hours: weekends by special appointment
  Facilities: tours, tasting, sales
  Winemaker: Keith D. Nelson
  Wines: varietal, generic, champagne
  Volume: 2,300 gallons fermenting, 7,000 gallons storage, 3,000 cases annually now, 14,000 eventually

WEIBEL CHAMPAGNE VINEYARDS   Page 183
  Address: 7051 North State St., Ukiah, Calif., 95470
  Phone: (707) 485-0321; home plant (415) 656-2340
  Hours: 10-6 daily
  Facilities: tasting, sales, gift shop, no tours
  Winemaker: Oscar Hableutzel
  Wines: varietal, generic, dessert, champagne, aperitifs
  Vineyards: 100 acres
  Volume: 50,000 gallons fermenting

Z-D WINERY   Page 81
  Address: 20735 Burndale Rd., Sonoma, Calif., 95476
  Phone: (707) 539-9137
  Hours: visits by appointment on weekends
  Facilities: tours and tasting by appointment only, sales
  Winemaker: Gino R. Zepponi & Norman C. de Leuze
  Wines: varietal
  Volume: 4,000 gallons fermenting, 7,000 gallons storage, 1,500 cases annually

FINIS